GOSPEL ORIGINS

STUDIES IN THEOLOGY

12mo, cloth.   75 cents net per vol.

NOW READY

A Critical Introduction to the New Testament
By ARTHUR SAMUEL PEAKE, D.D.

Faith and its Psychology
By the Rev. WILLIAM R. INGE, D.D.

Philosophy and Religion
By the Rev. HASTINGS RASHDALL, D.Litt. (Oxon), D.C.L. (Durham), F.B.A.

Revelation and Inspiration
By the Rev. JAMES ORR, D.D.

Christianity and Social Questions
By the Rev. WILLIAM CUNNINGHAM, D.D., F.B.A.

Christian Thought to the Reformation
By HERBERT B. WORKMAN, D.Litt.

Protestant Thought Before Kant
By A. C. MCGIFFERT, Ph.D., D.D.

An Outline of the History of Christian Thought Since Kant
By EDWARD CALDWELL MOORE, D.D.

The Christian Hope: A Study in the Doctrine of Immortality
By WILLIAM ADAMS BROWN, Ph.D., D.D.

The Theology of the Gospels
By the Rev. JAMES MOFFATT, D.D., D.Litt.

The Text and Canon of the New Testament
By ALEXANDER SOUTER, D.Litt.

A Critical Introduction to the Old Testament
By the Rev. GEORGE BUCHANAN GRAY, D.D., D.Litt.

A Handbook of Christian Apologetics
By ALFRED ERNEST GARVIE, M.A., D.D.

Gospel Origins
By the Rev. WILLIAM WEST HOLDSWORTH, M.A.

GOSPEL ORIGINS

A Study in the Synoptic Problem

BY THE REV.

WILLIAM WEST HOLDSWORTH, M.A.

TUTOR IN NEW TESTAMENT LANGUAGE AND LITERATURE
HANDSWORTH COLLEGE

AUTHOR OF 'THE CHRIST OF THE GOSPELS
'THE LIFE OF FAITH,' ETC.

NEW YORK
CHARLES SCRIBNER'S SONS
1913

I DEDICATE THIS WORK

TO THOSE BEST TEACHERS

MY STUDENTS

OF THE EAST AND OF THE WEST

Ἐπειδήπερ πολλοὶ ἐπεχείρησαν ἀνατάξασθαι διήγησιν περὶ τῶν πεπληροφορημένων ἐν ἡμῖν πραγμάτων, καθὼς παρέδοσαν ἡμῖν οἱ ἀπ' ἀρχῆς αὐτόπται καὶ ὑπηρέται γενόμενοι τοῦ λόγου, ἔδοξε κἀμοὶ, παρηκολουθηκότι ἄνωθεν πᾶσιν ἀκριβῶς, καθεξῆς σοὶ γράψαι, κράτιστε Θεόφιλε, ἵνα ἐπιγνῷς περὶ ὧν κατηχήθης λόγων τὴν ἀσφάλειαν.

St. Luke.

PREFACE

THE chapters which make up this little book are so many studies in the Synoptic Problem. The author makes no claim to originality in dealing with this question. He has made full use of the minute research and laborious work of those who have preceded him ; but he has tried to carry their work on to a further stage in endeavouring to define more closely than they have done the sources used by the three evangelists. In doing so he has given the fullest consideration to the many different theories advanced by modern scholars, and in consequence, though it cannot be claimed that this work is a ' Handbook ' on the subject with which it deals, yet the hope is cherished that students will be able, in following the line of thought advanced, to bring into view the several positions taken up by those who have attempted a solution.

The line followed in treating this subject was first suggested by the distinction made by Dr. Arthur Wright between the three editions of the Markan narrative which appear in the three Gospels as we know them, and Dr. Wright's well-known titles for these editions—proto-Mark, deutero-Mark, and trito-Mark—have been freely used in the pages which follow. The author, however, has ventured to differ from Dr. Wright in an important particular, in that he applies this differentiation not to an oral tradition, but to *documents*, and a study of the Gospels, extending

now over many years, from this point of view, has led
him to the conclusion that it offers the most likely solution
of the difficult but fascinating problem.   Should this conclusion be finally reached by others, the fullest acknow-
ledgment will be due to the distinguished scholar whose
Synopsis will long remain an indispensable text-book for
students of the Gospels.

But the recognition of a deutero-Mark in the first Gospel,
and an attempt to separate this element, has led the
author to a second conclusion, and this is that the Logia of
St. Matthew are not lost, as so many have thought, but
actually exist, sandwiched between distinctly Markan
sections, in the Gospel which bears St. Matthew's name.
This led to an attempt to define the source of the sayings
thus compiled by St. Matthew, a source generally indicated
by the formula ' Q.' Finally, when, in the case of the third
Gospel, the Markan section, or proto-Mark was removed,
together with the sections taken from Q thus defined,
the remainder appeared to possess so many common
features that it seemed possible to bring the whole of it
under one designation, and to ascribe it to a single authorship.   It is hoped that it may be seen that outstanding
features of the three Gospels may be fairly accounted for
in this way, and that the sources from which the three
evangelists derived their material afford a sufficient
guarantee for the deeds and words of Jesus as these appear
in the three Gospels.

In the hope that the book may be read by others than
students, critical details have been eliminated from the
main chapters.   They appear, however, in additional notes
attached to the several chapters, and it is hoped that in
considering the theory here advanced judgment will be

suspended until these last have been examined. Instead of crowding the pages with references to other works on the subject, it has been thought best to give a list of the works which have been freely used by the present author. His indebtedness to his many teachers is hereby fully acknowledged, and if he may venture to mention one name it shall be that of the scholar whose work in this department, as in others, has been both stimulus and example to a host of students unknown to him. The praise of Dr. Sanday is in all the Churches.

In conclusion, the author would express his great indebtedness to his friends, the Rev. J. A. Vanes, B.A., and Mr. F. Richards, M.A., for their most helpful suggestions made during the preparation of the work.

W. W. HOLDSWORTH.

HANDSWORTH COLLEGE,
January 1, 1913.

CONTENTS

CHAPTER I

The Synoptic Problem arises out of a study of prominent features of the first three Gospels.

These correspond so closely as to suggest a common origin.

Yet they also vary in a way which indicates a variety of sources.

Their production was governed by conditions existing in the Church of the first century.

They arose from the preaching of the first Apostles.

Both narrative and discourses must have appeared early in documentary form.

Each Gospel reveals a 'tendency' of its own.

This tendency illustrated from the three records of our Lord's teaching on the subject of divorce.

Such differences call for explanation. Theories which have been advanced.

Differences will be best accounted for if we succeed in going behind the canonical Gospels and defining their sources.

ADDITIONAL NOTE

Oral tradition as a basis for the Synoptic Gospels.

The oral theory of the origin of the Gospels.

The theory, though attractive, is not consistent, and fails to convince.

Reasons advanced for its failure.

CHAPTER II

The history of criticism.

'Harmonies' of the Gospels.

The sections of Ammonius and the canons of Eusebius.

Tatian's Diatessaron.

CHAPTER V

The first and third Gospels reproduce Markan narrative.
But they often differ from canonical Mark.
The theory of an Ur-Markus or original Mark.
Mark is homogeneous, and does not exhibit any dependence upon Q.
The ' Little Apocalypse ' in the second Gospel.
The absence of doublets from Mark.
The history of St. Mark.
Three editions of Markan narrative.
Vivid details indicate a later edition, not an earlier.
The secondary character of canonical Mark is further indicated by
its Pauline characteristics and such details as the use of the
word εὐαγγέλιον.
St. Mark's use of names.
The Latinisms of the second Gospel.
The date of the composition of the second Gospel.

ADDITIONAL NOTES

1. Analysis of the second Gospel, with notes.
2. The sayings of Jesus in the second Gospel.

CHAPTER VI

The Preface to the third Gospel.
The Markan source. How it came into the hands of St. Luke.
His treatment of this source. St. Luke's omissions.
The Logian document.
Additional sections :—
1. The Nativity story.
2. The travel document.
3. The history of the Passion and of the Resurrection.
Features common to these three and indicating a single source.

ADDITIONAL NOTES.

1. Analysis of the third Gospel.
2. St. Luke's ' special source.' Analysis, with notes.
3. The sayings of Jesus in St. Luke's Gospel.

CHAPTER VII

GOSPEL ORIGINS

CHAPTER I

APOSTOLIC PREACHING AND GOSPEL ORIGINS

THE four Gospels of the Christian Canon are usually
divided into two classes. The fourth Gospel is not only
independent of the other three : it differs in the personages
that appear in its pages, in the incidents recorded, and in
treatment. The Person of our Lord is set before us from
a point of view other than that which appears in the
Synoptic Gospels, and both His words and His works are
given us not merely with a different interpretation from
that which we have in the other Gospels, but in an entirely
different setting. This Gospel is therefore rightly placed
in a class by itself. But the remaining three are closely
connected. They exhibit a similar method of compilation.
They deal with the same facts in the history of Jesus, and
the words in which these are recorded correspond so
closely that it is impossible to consider that they are
independent one of another. They give us a common
view of our Lord, and for that reason they have received
the name of the Synoptic Gospels. The correspondence
between them is so close that the question of a common
origin is suggested as soon as we begin to compare them.
That correspondence, however, is not complete. Together
with points of closest similarity marked divergences
appear, and these last are so many and so distinct that
any attempt to refer the Gospels to a single source is
certain to break down.

Now the historical value, and the moral authority of any writing, is always dependent upon the character of its author, and the position which he occupies with reference to that which he describes or records. No writing in the world demands a clear presentation of authorship so much as do the Gospels upon which we rely for our conception of the Person of Christ, the central fact of the Christian religion. But directly we ask how did these all-important books come to be written, we are confronted with the difficulty that we have no contemporary writings which might have been expected to suggest to us those facts of authorship which we need to establish the tremendous claim which the writings make upon the judgment and the faith of men. We are driven then to the books themselves. But here, as we have already indicated, we find that though the main facts of authorship may be considered to be fairly established, the mutual relations of the matter which they use are far from clear. Sources are indicated ; some of these are distinctly seen ; others are obscure. The lines upon which we pursue our quest cross and recross, until the question of the sources of the three Gospels has become one of the most difficult of all the problems which confront the student of the New Testament.

In approaching the study of the Synoptic Gospels it is necessary to clear the mind of certain natural but misleading prepossessions. The writers, or editors, of these Gospels were men who worked under conditions belonging to their own age, and when we ask what these were, we are carried back to the latter half of the first century of the Christian era. Now in the governing idea of the Church of that time, as well as in its organisation and method of work, we may detect elements which were bound to influence any scheme of drawing up a narrative of the work and teaching of Jesus. We may go further and say that certain features of the life and outlook of the Church of the first century would even militate against the production of anything in the nature of 'history,' as we conceive it. Possessed, as its members were, with the expectation of the immediate return of their Lord, they would never dream that they were writing for all time, nor would they, like the Church of a later day, be troubled with the question whether this or that writing should be considered to be 'canonical.' To them 'the Scriptures' would mean what we call the Old Testament,' and the idea that they were creating what would rank as of equal authority with this, would never be entertained by them. They wrote, we may be sure, 'as the occasion demanded,' and that occasion might often be caused by some need which was distinctly personal or local.

Again, there was no special organic unity between the different centres of the Christian community. 'Churches' in those days had a distinctly local limitation. There was one in Rome, and another in Kenchraea, and several in the region known as 'Galatia.' The Church might even be found existing among the slaves who formed 'the household' of an individual. Among these scattered congregations there moved a number of men variously described as Apostles, Prophets (or Preachers) and Teachers. Their function was that of 'confirming' or 'building up' the individual Churches they visited. They did so, for the most part, by relating and explaining what Jesus had said or had done. Their qualification was found in some direct and immediate personal contact with the Lord. Their position was 'charismatic'—that is, it rested upon some gracious manifestation conferred upon them—and it was therefore privileged. St. Paul rested his claim to apostleship largely upon the fact that he had seen the Lord Jesus, and in such descriptions of his spoken ministry as are suggested to us in the course of his writing he seems to have dealt with the accepted facts of our

Lord's life. Writing to the Galatians he speaks of himself as having so described the death of Jesus that it was as if the Crucified had been depicted before their very eyes. His teaching of the Resurrection also had been clear and definite. It was in accordance with information which he had himself received from members of the apostolic band, doubtless on the occasion when he had ' interviewed ' Peter and James, the brother of the Lord, in Jerusalem (Gal. i. 18), but he claims that he was indebted more to personal revelation than to instruction from the other apostles. Such references to the oral teaching of the apostles lead to the inference that it did not lack that insistence upon guaranteed fact concerning the life and death of Jesus, which appears also in the recorded preaching of St. Peter in the Acts of the Apostles. We may accept that he also ' in the synagogues proclaimed Jesus, that He is the Son of God ' (Acts ix. 20). We are expressly told that such teaching was given not on any definite and consecutive plan. It would conform to the method ascribed to both St. Peter and his ' Interpreter,' St. Mark, the one in his preaching and the other as recording the preaching. For Eusebius quotes Papias in the following words : ' Mark having become the interpreter of Peter, wrote down accurately everything that he remembered, without, however, recording in order what was either said or done by Christ. For neither did he hear the Lord nor did he follow Him ; but afterwards attended Peter, who adapted his instructions to the needs of his hearers, but not as making a connected narrative of the Lord's discourses.' [1] This statement of Papias will come before us again, but it is mentioned here in support of the general statement that the early teaching of the Church out of which arose the documents to be considered was occasional rather than continuous, disconnected rather than systematic, and topical rather than historical. It

[1] Eusebius, *Hist.* iii. 39.

was also conditioned by local circumstances.   The needs of
his hearers could not be considered apart from their environment.   That which would be of interest to people in
Caesarea might be comparatively unimportant to those
who lived in Rome, so that we shall be prepared for a considerable amount of variation in the telling of the story.

This view of the circumstances in which the earliest
apostolic teaching was given is of importance in judging
whether the basis of the Gospel record was oral or not.
The advocates of this theory presuppose a fixed form of
narrative repeated frequently and without variation in
the selection of incidents, the order of their narration,
and the language employed, so as to lead to the ' stereotyping ' which they need to account for the marked
resemblance of the three Gospels.   We may well ask
where and how this fixed oral tradition came into being
if the earliest teaching lacked continuity, and depended
upon the varying needs of groups of Christians separated
in locality and to some extent in habit of thought and
interest.

We are told in the Didache, an important Church
manual composed about the end of the first century, and
dealing with the teaching of the twelve apostles, that the
' apostle ' moved on from place to place, and that he was
not to remain more than two days in one place (*Did.* xi. 5).
It is obvious that this would create another set of circumstances which would affect the question of Gospel origins.
How would the severed ἐκκλησίαι be instructed during
the intervals between one apostolical visitation and
another ?   Who would continue to them the recital of
what Jesus did and said, when the missionary had moved
on to some other Church ?   And what authority would
such a later recital possess ?   Their need would be met
in the most obvious manner by committing to writing the
authoritative statements made by those who had been
eye-witnesses of our Lord, and these documents might be

read by the local officers the bishops and deacons, as
described in the Didache. That this is what actually took
place is distinctly stated by Clement of Alexandria, who
says that 'When Peter had publicly preached the word
in Rome, and declared the Gospel by the Spirit, those who
were present, being many, urged Mark, as one who had
followed him for a long time and remembered what he
said, to record what he stated ; and that he having made
his Gospel gave it to those who made the request of him '
(*Hypotyp*. vi.). This is supported by a similar statement
in Eusebius (*Hist*. ii. 15), who says that Peter's hearers
were not content with the unwritten teaching of the
Gospel, but ' with all sorts of entreaties they besought
Mark, a follower of Peter, that he would leave with them
a written monument of the doctrine which had been
orally communicated to them. Nor did they cease until
they had prevailed with the man, and thus become the
occasion of the written Gospel which bears the name of
Mark.' We may be sure that the request made in Rome,
as Clement tells us, was one which would be made in other
places. Harnack quotes from Eusebius a statement to
the effect that the four daughters of Philip ' transmitted
stories of the old days,' a statement which accords with
the reference to the same women in the Acts of the Apostles
as being women ' who did prophesy.' Such references
will be most easily understood if we take them to indicate
that these women possessed written records of ' the old
days,' and that their ministry was found in reading and
expounding these to the local Church in Caesarea, in con-
tinuation of the practice of reading passages from the
Old Testament in the Synagogues of the Jews. The early
existence of such records may then be taken for granted.
Inasmuch as their subject-matter would be the same, they
would exhibit a marked resemblance to one another, but
inasmuch as they would arise to meet local necessities
there would also be equally marked differences.

The language in which they would be written would be that type of Greek which formed the spoken language of the common people ; for it is probable that the demand for such literature arose as soon as the Church began to appeal to those members of the community who are described in the Acts of the Apostles as consisting of ' devout persons ' (οἱ σεβόμενοι). These formed what has been called ' the seed-bed of Christianity.' They consisted of those Gentiles who were attracted by the teaching of the Jews and were in sympathy with their religion. Such a one was Cornelius, and we may well imagine that after St. Peter had delivered in his house the address recorded in the Acts of the Apostles, this would be written down by his interpreter, St. Mark, probably associated very early with St. Peter, and that it would be written not in Aramaic, but in such a language as would make it accessible to those for whom it was written.

Probably even before this there existed a number of those pointed apophthegms spoken by our Lord to which the name of ' Sayings ' (λόγια) would at once be given. This name would suggest itself because the very form of the sayings would suggest the oracular statements to which the name had long before been given. Such sayings would be received with peculiar reverence in the early Church. What could have been more precious than the very words of the Master Himself ? In their earliest form they would doubtless appear in Aramaic, but as soon as Christianity began to appeal to Gentiles the need of having these also in Greek would be felt, and more than one collection of them would be made by the devout. If we may accept the year A.D. 80 as being approximately the date of the composition of the third Gospel, it is clear that even then there were in existence many writings of which St. Luke had cognisance (Luke i. 1-4). It will later on be shown that the sayings used by St. Luke differed so markedly from those which appear in the first Gospel,

that it is most likely that he did not take them from the
first Gospel, but from some one of other collections, and
if there was any great multiplication of these the need
would be felt of making such a compilation of them as
might be considered authoritative. We shall be able to
account in this way for the tradition, to which reference
must presently be made, that St. Matthew compiled the
sayings of our Lord, and the fact of a collection made on
such authority would account for the disappearance of
others which did not possess such a guarantee.

As soon as we begin to read the three earlier Gospels,
we find that there is a considerable amount of repetition.
Incidents mentioned in one are repeated, often word for
word, in another. In many cases expressions which are
unusual,[1] words which are rare in writings related in time
to these Gospels, occur in all three. Not only so, but so
far as the narrative portion of these Gospels is concerned,
the general order of events is, speaking generally, the
same in each. We find also that with the possible
exception of the second Gospel the works are composite.
In the first Gospel and in the third it is possible to distinguish certain sections as narrative and others as consisting of discourses. The difference between the seventh
chapter of St. Matthew's Gospel and the eighth, or between
the sixth and seventh of St. Luke's, is unmistakable.
If we turn our attention for the moment to the narrative
sections of these two Gospels we observe a close correspondence between them and what we have in the second
Gospel, while in this last we find that the element of discourse, in the form in which it appears in the others, is

---

[1] The following unusual words are taken from Dr. Gould's Commentary
on Mark :—

πρωτοκαθεδρίας	*Matt. xxiii.* 6.	*Luke xi.* 43.	*Mark xii.* 39.
ἐκολόβωσε	*Mark xiii.* 20.	*Matt. xxiv.* 22.	
τέρατα	*Mark xiii.* 22.	*Matt. xxiv.* 25.	
ἀγρυπνεῖτε	*Mark xiii.* 33.	*Luke xxi.* 36.	
ἐμβάπτω }	*Mark xiv.* 20.	*Matt. xxvi.* 33.	
τρύβλιον }			

lacking. It has therefore become an accepted axiom with scholars that the narrative portion of both the first and the third Gospels is Markan. But it is not wholly Markan. There are considerable sections, especially in the third Gospel, which are distinctly narrative, but which do not appear either in Matthew or in Mark. They seem to be derived from quite another source. The composite character of Matthew and Luke is therefore accepted as readily as the derivation of their narrative portions from St. Mark.

We may here refer to the point of view of the several evangelists, or as it is nowadays called, the ' tendency,' and this must always be carefully borne in mind. It is one of the most important conditions governing the form of the several Gospels. In the first Gospel we find abundant references which indicate a distinctly Jewish tendency. The genealogy with which the Gospel opens begins with Abraham, while St. Luke, writing with Gentile sympathies, carries the genealogy up to Adam. Other features of the first Gospel indicating the same tendency, are the prominence given to Christ's teaching concerning the Messianic kingdom, the frequent use of Old Testament writings to prove the Messiahship of Jesus, references to Jerusalem as ' the holy city,' and the like. The second Gospel, on the other hand, is not so much concerned with the Messiahship of Jesus as with such a presentation of His Person as will prove Him to be the Son of God. St. Mark is at pains to explain Jewish words and customs, thus proving that he wrote with non-Jewish readers in view. The frequency with which he uses Latin words and military terms would seem to indicate—what indeed tradition declares—that he wrote for those who dwelt in Rome, and that soldiers were immediately interested in his writing (Clement of Alexandria, *Adumbr. in Pet.* Ep. i.). St. Luke, on the other hand, reveals all through the third Gospel the unmistakable marks of one who was closely

associated with St. Paul, and who reproduces not only
the characteristic phraseology of that apostle, but also
his world-wide view and strongly Gentile sympathies.
We shall also see, in his markedly sympathetic references
to women, a tendency which plays an important part in
enabling us to determine at least one of his sources.

Now the study of ' tendency ' will carry us a long way
in accounting for divergences between one gospel and
another where they relate the same incident or record the
same teaching, but it does not carry us all the way.   There
are differences in the common record which are not
accounted for by the principle of selection or expression
in this individual or in that, and an excellent illustration
of this is afforded by the several accounts of our Lord's
teaching on the subject of divorce.   In Mark x. 2-12 we
have the incident which gave rise to our Lord's pronouncement on the subject.   We are told that it arose from an
attempt made by the Pharisees to get our Lord to com-
promise Himself by a declaration which would contravene
the Mosaic directions.   This appears again in the Markan
section of the first Gospel which is given in Matthew xix.,
but in this last we find a considerable amount of variation
from the account given in Mark, and the differences between
the two accounts are precisely those which would occur
when the same person repeated what he had written in a
former edition.   There is a difference in the order of the
several statements on the subject, and the account in
the second Gospel is considerably abbreviated.   If we
consider that the second Gospel is prior to the first, we
are bound to accept what seems most unlikely, namely,
that the evangelist of the first Gospel made considerable
additions to the Markan narrative in transcribing from
that source.   The third Gospel, on the other hand, does
not record the Markan section at all, and if that Gospel
was based upon canonical Mark we shall ask why St.
Luke decided to omit it.   It cannot be because he thought

the teaching inappropriate to his particular line of thought in composing his Gospel, for he has included the same teaching in a passage which he derived from the Logia, where he gives our Lord's words without any of those qualifications which we have in the first Gospel. Nor can we suppose that for the sake of abbreviation he could omit the whole passage. A better explanation of the facts is that this section was not in the Markan edition used by St. Luke.

But in addition to this section in the Markan narrative we have our Lord's words given again in the Sermon on the Mount in the first Gospel and in the Travel Document in the third. Here the words are given in the form of a Logion. That is, there is no attempt to connect the utterance with any incident in the history. It is cast in epigrammatic form. It possesses all the characteristics of a true Logion.[1] But when we come to consider the Lukan version in comparison with that given in the first Gospel, we see at once that it is difficult to believe that the two evangelists derived the saying from Q or any other common document. We are bound to admit that here the sources were different. The two passages should be placed in parallel columns:

It was said also whosoever shall put away his wife let him give her a writ of divorcement: but I say unto you, that every one that putteth away his wife, saving for the cause of fornication, maketh her an adulteress; and whosoever shall marry her when she is put away committeth adultery.

Matt. v. 31-32.

Every one that putteth away his wife and marrieth another committeth adultery, and he that marrieth one that is put away from a husband committeth adultery.

Luke xvi. 18.

It is difficult to believe that the considerable difference

[1] See p. 41.

between the two statements can be explained on the
ground of editorial alterations. As we shall see, St. Luke
treats his Logian source with such respect that he makes
such alterations less frequently in this part of his Gospel
than he does in any other. We are shut up to the conclusion
that the sayings were taken from different sources, and the
emphasis in the Lukan account upon the man's action in
the matter would seem to indicate a woman's point of
view. There is also the significant addition in the
Matthaean version of the clause ' saving for the cause
of fornication.' Why did St. Luke omit this clause if he
used the same source as St. Matthew did ? We may be
sure that it was not in the saying as he found it in his
collection of Logia. Indeed, the fact that it appears in
the first Gospel seems to indicate that it must be considered to be inserted by St. Matthew as an interpretation
of the spirit of our Lord's teaching on the subject, and as
a concession made to the Jewish Christian Church for
which he wrote. That Church would find it difficult to
break away all at once from the Mosaic statute on the
subject, and the qualifying clause would be added ' for
the hardness of their hearts.' It is to be noticed that it
appears only in the first Gospel, and that it is inserted
in the Markan section of this Gospel as well as in the
Sermon on the Mount. The use of the word πορνεία
again is significant and points in the same direction. It
is not ' fornication ' as an act common to the two sexes
which is indicated as the one exception. πορνεία describes
rather the professional harlotry of women. So that the
exception is made in the interests of men just as was the
case in the Mosaic law given in Deuteronomy xxiv. 1.

The above study of the facts before us in the record show
that, while tendency may account for the character of those
points in which the first Gospel reveals an addition to what
we have in the second, it does not account for the omission
by St. Luke of a section which certainly belongs to the

Markan narrative, nor does it account for the difference between the teaching of our Lord on the subject which he derived from his second source and that given by St. Matthew, and apparently derived from a similar source. The only complete explanation of the facts will be found when we accept the theory that the Markan source used by the first and third evangelists was not identical with canonical Mark, and that the collection of ' Sayings ' used by St. Luke differed from that which was used by St. Matthew.   When we further discover that this theory accounts for a large number of other differences between one Gospel and another, we may feel a considerable amount of confidence in applying the theory to the general question of Gospel sources.

There are of course other explanations of the facts with which we have to deal, and these must be fully weighed by the student of the Gospels.   One of the most recent of these is given by Dr. Sanday in a work to which frequent reference will be made in subsequent chapters.   Dr. Sanday describes the several evangelists as being historians rather than mere transcribers of other matter that came before them, and as exercising a certain amount of freedom in selecting from their material that which seemed to be of importance from their several points of view.   ' They were faithful and yet independent ; not wilfully capricious, but content to tell their story sometimes in the words of their predecessors, sometimes in their own.   Their method in transcribing would to a large extent be formed by the conditions under which they worked, and consequently the evangelist, in reproducing what belonged to his source, would trust largely to his memory.   This will perhaps explain the fact that, while there is a considerable amount of agreement where Markan matter appears in the first and third Gospels, there is also a great amount of divergence.' [1]   Now it is possible that this may be the

[1] *Oxford Studies in the Synoptic Problem.*

explanation of the facts under consideration ; but while it might account for merely verbal divergences, it fails altogether to account for the omission in one Gospel of a whole incident, or for the inclusion in another of a considerable block of matter. For example, the omission by St. Luke of the story of the cure of the Syrophenician's daughter could not be accounted for in this way. It is impossible to believe that if St. Luke had come upon that story in his source he could ever have forgotten it. Some other explanation of the fact has therefore to be discovered. Some of these are discussed in another chapter, but it is possible that most, if not all, of these divergences from the Markan tradition may be due to the simple fact that they were not included in the editions of Mark used by the editors of the first and third Gospels. This theory will be fully discussed later on, but in considering the conditions under which the different evangelists prepared their work, we must not lose sight of the possibility that the copies from which they worked were not identical. Dr. Sanday would account for ' by far the greater number of the coincidences of Matthew-Luke against Mark as being due to the use by Matthew-Luke of a recension of the text of Mark different from that from which all the extant MSS. of the Gospel are descended.' Again, we would urge that while this is possible, other explanations of the facts should first be tested before we draw such a conclusion. It involves, for instance, what seems a very unlikely thing to happen, viz. that ' this recension was perpetuated in just these two copies, but after giving birth to them it came to an abrupt end ' : this statement is actually made by Dr. Sanday in his Essay in the *Oxford Studies in the Synoptic Problem.*

Rejecting then the theory that divergences from the second Gospel are to be explained by the supposition that the evangelist failed to carry in his memory the whole of the section he was transcribing, and rejecting also that they are to be explained on the ground of a recension of the text, we find another attempt made to account for them on the ground that they are due to editorial alterations. For example, it is well known that the word εὐθύς occurs with extraordinary frequency in the second Gospel, appearing no less than forty-two times. In Matthew it occurs only six times, and in Luke in a single passage taken from the Logia document and not from Mark. Now while the marked absence of the word from the third Gospel may be due to St. Luke's dislike of the word, yet when we find that the editor of the first Gospel also rejects it in thirty-six passages, we are led to think that the explanation must be sought elsewhere than in the direction of editorial alteration. For it is most unlikely that two editors, one of them a Jew and the other a Gentile, working separately with very different constituencies before them, would agree in omitting this word so often. But if canonical Mark differs from other Markan narrative in this that it was later than they, then we can see that everything that tended to make an incident more vivid would appear in the later edition though it was not found in the earlier.

Few will care to deny a considerable amount of editorial alteration in the dealing of these editors with their material. While in the main they were faithful to the sources which they used, they nevertheless allowed themselves considerable freedom in substituting words which seemed more suitable to them, and in recasting phrases which appeared to them to be imperfectly expressed. But to press this principle so far as to hold that it explains the many cases in which Matthew and Luke agree against Mark seems to be a mistake. A far more likely line of investigation is that in which an attempt is made to go behind the evangelists whose work we have in the canonical Gospels, and bearing in mind the conditions in which the work of the earliest preachers was accomplished,

to ask whether we can say anything more definite than, ' a
Gospel practically identical with our second Gospel ' when
speaking of Markan narrative, and anything which will
indicate the second documentary source more certainly
than the very indefinite Q. Such questions may well
be considered now.   An enormous amount of research
has been accomplished, and in so far as an agreement has
been reached that all three Gospels are not at all original
productions but rest upon previously existing documents,
the ground has been cleared for the further question
whether those documents can be more fully defined.   There
is no reason why we should approach this question with
a feeling of despair. We have certain statements in
Patristic writings to guide us. It is true that these have
often seemed so contradictory of one another that little
use has been made of their statements, and perhaps the
impatience which has been felt with regard to anything
that savoured of ' the traditional view ' may have con-
tributed to the neglect of this part of the evidence for
Gospel origins.   But there is a feeling in the present time
that there is more to be said on the side of ' tradition,' and
it may be that our own prepossessions have had much to
do with the mutual contradictions which we discover in
the writings of the fathers.   There is, for instance, a
tradition which connects the second Gospel with Egypt,
another connects it with Rome. We have too hastily
said ' both cannot be right,' and dismissed the writings
as being to this extent untrustworthy. And yet we hope
to show that there is a sense in which both these statements are correct. The true method of investigation is
that in which neither internal nor external evidence is
neglected, but the one is tested by the other, and it may
well be that following this method we may arrive at what
is of supreme importance to the Church at the present day.
For if the Gospels as we have them are secondary, that is,
if the writers derived them from other sources, so that the

part they played was rather editorial than original, we shall only establish the authority of the Gospels in so far as we see that those who first compiled the writings were in a position to guarantee the statements they have made.

ADDITIONAL NOTE

THE THEORY OF ORAL TRADITION AS A BASIS FOR THE SYNOPTIC GOSPELS

In describing the conditions under which the evangelists worked, we have so far proceeded on the supposition that the sources from which they drew their matter were documentary. This is now largely accepted by scholars both in Germany and in England.   Justice must, however, be done to a theory which at one time seemed to promise a full solution of the Synoptic Problem.   Towards the end of the eighteenth century G. Herder put forward a theory that all three Gospels were based upon another Gospel which, though fixed in form, only existed in an unwritten tradition.   This Gospel originated in Palestine and was written in Aramaic, forming the content of apostolic preaching, and it was communicated frequently in the schools of Catechumens into which new converts were gathered.   The fixity of this Gospel was accounted for as due at once to the catechetical method and to the development of memory which followed, and which can be amply illustrated from Eastern parallels.   St. Mark was the first to reduce this unwritten Gospel to writing, and later on another version of the same was produced which eventually became our Gospel of St. Matthew. Later still St. Luke, using this Aramaic Gospel, and working over St. Mark's version which by that time had been published in Greek, prepared the Gospel which now bears his name.

This theory was developed by J. C. L. Giesler, who held that even in its Greek form the Gospel continued to be oral, and supported the theory by historical considerations, such as the absence of all allusions in the Gospels themselves to written documents, while the absence also of literary culture in the early Church made it unlikely that the Gospel would assume a written form.   In England this theory was advocated by Dr.

Westcott, and later on by Dr. Arthur Wright, whose *Synopsis of the Gospels* in Greek remains to-day the most able presentation of the theory.

The doctrine of an oral basis for the Gospels is at first sight exceedingly attractive. It fits in admirably with the method of instruction which to this day is pursued in Eastern countries, and the element of stereotyping which it assumes seems to offer a reasonable account of the extraordinarily close correspondence to be discovered between the three Gospels based upon it. In spite of this, however, it has failed to carry conviction, and is practically rejected both in Germany and in England.[1] Dr. Schmiedel speaks of the hypothesis as being at once an 'asylum ignorantiae,' and an 'asylum orthodoxiae.' He says it spares the critic all necessity for an answer to the question why one evangelist wrote in this manner and another in that. 'If the Synoptical oral narrative was really so firmly fixed as to secure verbatim repetition of entire verses in three authors writing independently of one another, then the variations between the three become all the more mysterious.' It is further a relief to the orthodox mind because 'it dispenses with the necessity of assuming that original documents from which our Gospels had been drawn—writings of eye-witnesses —have perished. The theory is really wrecked, as Dr. Schmiedel suggests, on the *differences* between one record and the other. Its advocates account for these on the ground that equally credible witnesses would give a different account of the same event, and memory might fail in transmitting orally the same discourse. But it is evident that the two terms of the hypothesis cancel one another. Its advocates cannot have it both ways. They claim 'a stereotyped tradition,' yet with it they allow for 'slips of memory.' If the tradition was so fixed as it must have been to account for the many and marked resemblances, such slips would have been impossible. Nor are these differences slight verbal changes. They amount in some cases to whole sections, and sections of great importance, such as the Lord's Prayer, the Eucharistic words, and the story of the Resurrection. If any sections in the Gospel story were likely to be fixed by frequency of repetition, they are these; yet we find that it is precisely in these that the account varies

---

[1] See Article *sub. verb.* 'Gospels' in the *Encyclopædia Biblica.*

most, and in each some detail which appears in the others is altogether missing. The hypothesis of an oral basis rests in reality upon the assumption that documents containing memoirs of the works and words of Jesus were comparatively late in appearing, but the existence of Logia preserved upon pieces of papyrus shows that there were documents at a very much earlier stage of Church history. So also does St. Paul's instructions with reference to the parchments which he so specially required during his imprisonment at Rome. St. Luke's language in the introduction to the third Gospel indicates that, even before he began to write, accounts of our Lord's life were extant in documentary form. (See p. 145.)

Again, the original instruction of converts, which we may well agree was given in catechetical form, must have been given in Aramaic, the mother-tongue of the first apostles, while these resemblances are in Greek, and it is difficult to believe that the same fixity in verbal expression would persist through the whole process of translation. An even more destructive criticism of this theory is to be found when we reflect that though this method of instruction must have arisen in Jerusalem, and though it is clear from the fourth Gospel, as well as from indications in the Synoptic Gospels, that there was a Judaean as well as a Galilean ministry in the course of our Lord's public life, yet this tradition scarcely refers at all to what took place in Judaea. 'The fact that the Synoptic Gospels record only the Galilean ministry is inexplicable if the tradition grew up in the heart of the city they so strangely neglected.'[1] In another passage of the same article Dr. Sanday says, 'The stamp which these Gospels bear is not collective but individual, and this cannot be explained if they are the product of the Church working collectively.' Such arguments make the theory of a purely oral tradition as the basis of the three Gospels untenable.

[1] See Article by Dr. Sanday in *The Expositor*, Fourth Series, iii. p. 186 ff. For a full and clear discussion of this subject, the student is referred to Dr. Stanton's work, *The Gospels as Historical Documents*, vol. ii. p. 17 ff. See also *Oxford Studies*, pp. 98, 99.

CHAPTER II

THE SYNOPTIC GOSPELS—THE HISTORY OF CRITICISM

THE four Gospels came into regular use in Church services
in the first quarter of the second century, and as soon as
they were thus put together it became evident that there
was much matter common to two, three, or even to four
Gospels. It was also seen that with this large body of
'similarities' there was a considerable amount of
'divergences.' The many attempts to deal with these
are so many efforts to solve what has become known as
'the Synoptic Problem.' Some methods adopted may
be at once dismissed as unscientific. While no attempt
was made to account for the points of correspondence, and
any recognition of the dependence of one evangelist upon
another was resented as a charge of plagiarism, the issue
of which would be the weakening of the authority of
Scripture, the differences existing between one Gospel and
another were explained away through fear of disclosing
contradiction between one record and another. This
attempt to resolve the variations existing in the several
stories was dignified by the name of 'harmonising,' and
the methods adopted by some harmonists are not such as
to raise them in public esteem, or add to the authority of
Scripture.

Even the text of Scripture has in not a few instances
been tampered with in the attempt to reduce the several
accounts to conformity, and textual critics have come
to recognise a whole class of readings as due to this
tendency, and quite rightly they make short work of such
variants. Harmonists of this class seem strangely to

ignore the fact that, so far from weakening the force and the authority of the record, the acceptance of divergences really increases these, inasmuch as it gives us the story from more than one point of view. The word ' harmony ' was indeed ill chosen by those who aimed at conformity, for the blending together of different notes, under well-defined laws, is what a true ' harmony ' really means. Reduction to a single expression might give us unison ; it certainly does not produce a harmony. In later days the word ' synopsis ' has come to be used instead of ' harmony,' and this secures the great advantage of indicating that in such work an attempt is made to bring the whole of the matter dealt with into the range of a single view, the student accepting divergences no less than similarities, and seeking to discover their significance.

In the third century Ammonius prepared a work in which the sections of the other Gospels were compared with those which appear in St. Matthew's Gospel, the text of which was given in full. The first Gospel thus became his basis, and the other Gospels were arranged in parallel columns where, in his opinion, the accounts coincided. He found in this way that Matthew contained 355 sections, Mark 233, Luke 342, and John 232. It is clear that such a method, while it had the advantage of bringing together similar passages, and of thus allowing comparison of their details, suffered from the disadvantage of being arbitrary in so far as the selection of parallels was concerned ; it broke up the text of all the Gospels with the exception of Matthew, and we do not know that it led to any criticism of the details thus arranged. It seems to have been rather a selection of parallel passages, than an attempt to deal with the Synoptic Problem. The splitting up of the Gospels other than Matthew seems to have been felt by Eusebius to be a defect, and he therefore, while making use of his predecessor's work, proceeded to number the sections in each Gospel. The sections thus

distinguished were called τὰ παραπλήσια, and in addition
to these Eusebius drew up a set of tables κανόνες in
which the numbers of the corresponding sections were
arranged together. References to these were made by
figures written on the margin of the text. These ' canons '
were prepared as follows : No. 1 contains a list of 71 places
in which all four Gospels agree. Nos. 2, 3, 4 show a list
of passages in which three have common matter amounting
to 158. Nos. 5, 6, 7, 8, 9 contain 141 passages in which
two have common matter and No. 10 consists of a list
of 62 passages peculiar to some one evangelist. The
method of using these canons was as follows : if any one
wished to consult the passages which were parallel to one
which he was reading, he would look at the margin and
see that the section number was accompanied by another
number indicating the table to which his passage belonged ;
turning to this table he would find opposite to the number
of the passage he was reading the numbers which indicated
the parallels in the other Gospels, and would thus be able
to consult them. This method, however, like that which
it was intended to supersede, is rather an arrangement of
parallel passages than a synopsis.

Another notable harmony was that prepared in the
second century by the Syrian Christian named Tatian.
Strictly speaking this was not a harmony at all, but rather
a Gospel narrative formed by selecting from all the Gospels
passages which seemed to follow one another consecutively.
Eusebius speaks somewhat contemptuously of this as
' a sort of connection or compilation, I know not how,
of the Gospels.' [1] Theodoret also speaks of the mischief
done by this ' Diatessaron,' as it is called, and congratu-
lates himself on the fact that having found some two
hundred copies of the work in one district of his diocese,
he was able to put them away and to replace them with

[1] συνάφειάν τινα καὶ συναγωγὴν οὐκ οἶδ' ὅπως τῶν εὐαγγελίων ; see Zahn,
i. pp. 14, 15.

Gospels of the four evangelists. It is possible that the Sinaitic and Curetonian texts of the Syriac version of the New Testament came into existence as the result of an attempt to destroy Tatian's work. The Diatessaron is of extreme importance from the standpoint of the textual critic, but it is clear that while the name given to it seems to suggest some attempt at harmonising the four Gospels, in reality it was not so at all, and for our purposes need not be further considered.

From the time when the Gospels began to circulate or to be appealed to, it was the common tradition of the Christian Church that they were written by those whose names they bear. Even Marcion, who took exception to many things which were stated in the Gospels, especially to statements made in the third, and did not hesitate to remove from the letters of St. Paul passages which he considered to be unauthorised and false, never attempted to question the authorship of the three books under consideration. This tradition rested upon no claim made within the books themselves, and the only possible explanation of it is that the tradition rested upon facts so clearly within the cognisance of the Christian Church that denial of the received authorship was held to be impossible. This tradition does not decide anything as to what we call ' the Synoptic Problem.' That is to say, it does not pronounce any opinion as to whether the books were entirely or only in part the work of the evangelists whose names they bear, neither does it say whether the writers wrote at first hand, or whether they were dependent upon others. The earliest titles were apparently those which appear in the oldest codices, and such forms as κατὰ Ματθαῖον, κατὰ Μάρκον might be used without reference to the dependence of the first Gospel on the second, or of St. Mark upon St. Peter. The early tradition says nothing as to ' Gospel sources.'

In certain codices the books appear in the order Matthew,

Mark, Luke, but Clement of Alexandria [1] held that St. Luke compiled the third Gospel before St. Mark wrote the second. The dates to which these Gospels may be assigned will be considered later in this chapter, but this divergence of opinion is to be noted here, for if it can be shown that St. Luke used an edition of St. Mark's work other than that which we have in canonical Mark, and written at an earlier date, the apparent contradiction may be easily resolved. Irenaeus,[2] too, represents St. Mark as having written his Gospel after the death of both St. Peter and St. Paul. If the third Gospel appeared before the death of the latter—and it is difficult to believe that St. Luke could have closed the account given in the Acts as he has done if St. Paul was not still alive—then the statement of Irenaeus must be held to refer to canonical Mark, a previous edition of that Gospel, differing in details but similar in arrangement and in many particulars even identical, having come into the hands of St. Luke. The order in which the books appear in the different codices cannot be held to be conclusive as to historical sequence. For the books would first be written on separate rolls and kept together. When they were put in the form of a codex the order in which they appeared would be quite adventitious. This is shown by the fact that codices which keep the traditional order for the Synoptic Gospels put the fourth Gospel before them all.

The first attempt to decide on the interdependence of the three Gospels was made by St. Augustine. He held that St. Matthew was the first to write and that St. Mark ' eum subsecutus tanquam pedisequus et abbreviator ejus videtur.' [3] He also held that St. Luke used both Matthew and Mark. This view obtained for a very long time, and it was not until the eighteenth century, when historical questions began to be treated upon scientific lines, that it

---

[1] Eus., *H.E.*, vi. 14. [2] Irenaeus, iii. 1, 1; Eus., *H.E.*, v. 8, 2.
[3] *De Consensu Ev.*, i. 2, 4.

was given up. Both in Germany and in England very different views have been held, and some attempt must be made to show the history of criticism.[1]

The first to offer any account of Gospel origins other than that of Augustine was G. E. Lessing, who held that the original Gospel was written in Aramaic, and that the three canonical Gospels are translations of this, the first Gospel coming nearest to the original. Lessing seems to have arrived at this conclusion by a rendering of the passage already quoted from Eusebius.[2]

Lessing was followed by J. J. Griesbach, who taught that St. Matthew wrote his Gospel from his own personal knowledge of Christ, and that St. Luke supplemented this from oral tradition, the second Gospel being made up of excerpts from the other two.

G. Herder seems to have been the first to see that the second Gospel must be considered prior to the other two. He held that St. Mark wrote down for his own convenience the teaching which had been given him orally, and that he did this at a quite early date, that later on an Aramaic Gospel was prepared and has survived in the first Gospel, and was used also by St. Luke, who added that which he had himself received from apostolic teachers.

A notable addition to criticism was made by J. C. L. Giesler, who found the common basis of the Synoptic Gospel in an oral tradition. This need not be further mentioned here, as we have already considered it in the Additional Note to chapter i. Another typical theory is that of B. Weiss. This theory had its antecedent in Eichhorn's, which again is based on that of Lessing noticed above. All of these, while they differ from one another, seek for the source of the Synoptic Gospels in an original Gospel written in Aramaic but early translated into Greek. This Gospel was held to consist for the most

[1] For the whole of this section I have used Zahn's *Intro. to the New Testament*, vol. ii.   [2] *Hist.* iii. 24, 6.

part of discourses, but it also contained narratives, and it may therefore be considered a ' Gospel,' and the Canonical Gospels are accounted for as translations, other supplementary matter being added as each translation was made. Thus the second Gospel was derived from this original Gospel with additions derived by St. Mark from the preaching of St. Peter. The first Gospel used the original and drew additional matter from St. Mark, and the third Gospel is based upon the original, St. Mark, and special sources available to St. Luke. This theory was a great advance upon all that had then appeared, but it is open to the serious objection discussed in connection with the question of an ' Ur-Markus ' in chapter v., and further, while it accounts fairly well for resemblances, it breaks down in attempting to account for divergences. For it is not merely in the supplementary matter that these appear, but even when common matter is being narrated by the different evangelists there are differences which are hard to explain if they had before them an original Gospel from which each was transcribing.

It is impossible here to pass in review the many attempts which have been made to solve the Synoptic Problem. The most that can be done is to select those which seem typical of groups, and we therefore turn to a theory which, with modifications, forms the basis of the present work. It is that of Holtzmann, who held that there were two documentary sources before the evangelists. One of these was Markan, and in its original form was used both by the editor who compiled the first Gospel and also by St. Luke. It was not quite identical with the second Gospel. The latter was considerably abbreviated, especially in the earliest section which forms an introduction. The account of the healing of the servant of the Centurion (Matt. viii. 5-13, Luke vii. 1-10) and other incidents were omitted. But additions to the original account were made in what is now canonical Mark, such as the cure of the deaf man

with an impediment in his speech (Mark vii. 32-37), and
the many vivid details which characterise the second
Gospel. The second document consists mainly of discourses, and is to be found most clearly in the third Gospel,
though the Church has acknowledged their author by
attaching his name to the first Gospel rather than the
third. Other material, such as the genealogies, derived
neither from St. Mark nor from the Logia, was added to
the first and third Gospels by their respective editors.
It is claimed that this hypothesis is in accord with the
statements of Papias already quoted. This theory has
not hitherto received any great amount of acceptance,
though there have been approximations to it in the course
of time. These will be noted when the question of the
Markan narrative is more fully before us.

Looking back over this necessarily imperfect survey of
the course of German criticism we may sum up results as
follows :—

1. The basis is held to be documentary rather than oral.
2. The basis is twofold, consisting largely of sayings and
   of narrative.
3. The former of these is connected with the name of
   St. Matthew, and the latter with that of St. Mark,
   and both of these in some form or other were used
   by St. Luke.

Beyond this point, however, there does not seem to be
any general consensus of opinion. The details vary
with the critic. When we turn to the course of English
criticism, we find that the general results of German
research are freely accepted, but here again, beyond the
three points mentioned above, there seems to be an almost
endless variety of opinion.

Giesler's theory of an oral basis from which all three
Canonical Gospels are derived is still maintained by Dr.
Arthur Wright. In a recent article in the *Expository*

Times (February 1910) he so far modifies his position as to allow that ' documents—temporary documents—were in use from the first ' ; but he finds these documents in tablets, ' perhaps half a dozen which St. Peter used for refreshing his memory.' This concession, however, is hardly sufficient, and it is difficult to imagine St. Peter ' using notes ' as a modern preacher might do.

In 1884 a work appeared under the names of Dr. Edwin A. Abbott and Mr. W. G. Rushbrooke, entitled *The Common Tradition of the Synoptic Gospels*. In this it was held that the basis of the three Gospels was to be discovered by ruling out everything except that which appeared in all three Gospels. When this is done, the remainder consists of briefest notes as terse as the wording of ' a modern telegram,' and the necessary expansion, before these could be worked up into the Gospels as we have them, accounts for the divergences which exist between them. This system of discovering the basis or bases of the Gospels is altogether too mechanical. The nucleus which results is called by the authors ' the Triple Tradition,' but it is clear that, inasmuch as the common matter may have come from one source, a better name would be that of ' the Original Tradition,' [1] and even thus it would fail to account for many of the peculiar features of these Gospels. The expansions, for instance, reveal a considerable amount of correspondence, and this fact becomes inexplicable if the three editors were expanding independently of one another.

The theory of an Ur-Markus, or original Gospel corresponding most closely to the second Gospel, is supported by Dr. Salmon, who holds that ' Matthew and Luke did not copy Mark, but that all drew from a common source, which, however, is represented most fully and with most verbal exactness in St. Mark's version.' Dr. Salmon thinks that it is even possible that St. Mark's Gospel may

[1] See Salmon, *Introduction*, etc., pp. 132 ff.

be the latest of the three, since it contains a good deal more than the Petrine tradition. This is an important concession from the point of view of the present work ; for if canonical Mark is later than the Markan narrative which appears in the first and third Gospels, it would account for those features which have thus impressed Dr. Salmon. The question of an Ur-Markus will receive separate treatment in a later chapter. [1] In addition to this Dr. Salmon assumes the existence of Matthaean Logia upon which the first and third Gospels are based.

The ninth edition of Dr. Salmon's *Introduction to the New Testament* was published in 1899, and since then we have had at least three works in English to which we must give some attention.

The first is that of Dr. Burkitt, entitled *The Gospel History in Transmission*, and published in 1906. Dr. Burkitt does not accept either the theory of oral tradition as a basis, or that of an Ur-Markus. He holds that ' the main common source of the Synoptic Gospels was a single written document.' This document he finds in canonical Mark. He follows Wellhausen in the belief that with one exception ' Mark was known to both the other synoptists in the same form and with the same contents as we have it now.' The one exception which Dr. Burkitt makes is that of the Eschatological Discourse (Mark xiii. 3-37), which he considers to differ in literary form from the rest of the Gospel, and regards as a separate ' fly-sheet ' incorporated by the evangelist, with or without alteration, into his work. He considers the Matthaean contribution to the first Gospel to be not the Logia, the reconstruction of which he holds to be hopeless, but a collection of Messianic proof-texts drawn up by Matthew the publican, and taken for the most part direct from the Hebrew. These Messianic texts were probably the Logia of which Papias, as quoted by Eusebius, speaks, and which

[1] See p. 107.

'each one interpreted as he could.' The non-Markan portions of the first and third Gospels he holds to belong to a work now lost, to designate which he adopts the convenient formula 'Q.'[1] Many of the positions here taken up will be discussed under the several headings to which they belong. We are concerned here with the mere statement of them.

In 1909 Dr. V. H. Stanton published a volume of extra-ordinary value for those who would study 'the Synoptic Problem.' It is entitled *The Gospels as Historical Documents*, vol. ii., and it is a clear and balanced statement of the many questions that arise in this connection. Dr. Stanton mentions the following as ' positions in regard to which a large amount of agreement has been attained ' :—

1. The resemblances between the Synoptic Gospels are such as require us to suppose connections through Greek sources.
2. The relations between the first three Gospels cannot be adequately explained by the influence of oral tradition.
3. Our third evangelist was not to any considerable extent dependent upon the first (or the first upon the third) for the common contents of their Gospels.
4. A record which, if not virtually identical with our St. Mark, is at least most nearly represented in it, was largely used in the composition of our first and third Gospels.
5. There was a second principal source common to our first and third evangelists, consisting mainly of discourses and sayings of Jesus, which they inde-pendently combined with their Markan document.

Dr. Stanton finds a considerable amount of freedom in amending the Markan document on the part of both the first and the third evangelists, and this may be readily

[1] See pp. 38 ff.

allowed. It is possible, however, that some things which
look like editorial emendations may be due to the fact that
the editions of St. Mark used by these other evangelists
differed from that which appears in canonical Mark.
Dr. Stanton himself seems to recognise this, though he
makes no clear pronouncement on the subject. Thus,
in discussing Markan sections omitted from the first
Gospel, he speaks of the possibility of their having been
absent from the copy of St. Mark which the evangelist was
using, and the agreements of Matthew and Luke against
Mark are accounted for as belonging to ' an earlier form of
Markan document.' This explanation he prefers to that
advanced by B. Weiss, that they indicate an 'Apostolic
Gospel,' containing both Logia and narrative, and drawn
upon by all three of our evangelists. On the other hand,
he speaks of the omission of the healing of the demoniac in
Matthew as having been due to mere inadvertence. Again
he accounts for the description of Jesus in Mark vi. 3, as
' the carpenter,' whereas Matthew has ' the son of the
carpenter ' (xiii. 55), and Luke ' the son of Joseph ' (iv. 22),
by ascribing the first-named to ' a revising hand,' and
where St. Mark has the expression ' servant of all ' (Mark
ix. 35), the phrase is accounted for as having been introduced by a copyist ' owing to his familiarity with other
sayings of our Lord.' In Mark xi. 17 the words ' for all
the nations,' wanting in Matthew and Luke, ' may have
been supplied from a recollection of the passage of the
prophet, and a sense of their significance.'

So in dealing with St. Luke's revision of his Markan
document, Dr. Stanton says that St. Luke, ' while adhering
closely on the whole to St. Mark's narrative, seems to
have here and there drawn inferences from what he read,
to have formed his own idea of the circumstances and
incidents, and then to have told the facts as he conceived
them. Or again, the special interest which he felt in the
subject-matter, and the belief that he could improve the

presentation of it, have moved him to add various touches
or to rearrange the account. Or, once more, some little
piece of additional information which he possessed, or a
different mode of telling a story to which he had become
accustomed, has exercised an influence upon him.'

Now while the possibility of these motives cannot be
denied, yet most, if not all, of such departures from the
Markan narrative seem to be better accounted for on the
supposition that they were not ' departures ' at all, and that
the real variation is in St. Mark's method of telling stories
which he repeated more than once. Thus it is well known
that though St. Luke is fond of the word used for ' preaching the Gospel '—as indeed a follower of St. Paul was
likely to be—he never uses the word ' Gospel.' And yet
the word is used absolutely in several passages occurring
in the second Gospel. Dr. Stanton accounts for the non-
appearance of this word in the third Gospel by suggesting
that the text of the second Gospel was altered so as to
allow for the insertion of the word. But we prefer the
theory that canonical Mark is a later edition of the Markan
narrative which St. Luke used, and that during the time
that had intervened between the publication of the two
editions the teaching of the Church had assumed the more
definite form of a Gospel. It therefore appears in
canonical Mark, but not in St. Luke's Gospel.[1]

Other examples bearing upon this point will be given in
a subsequent chapter, and we shall only say here that a
more thorough development of the theory of different
editions of the Markan document may possibly afford a
better explanation. In another passage Dr. Stanton
says : ' There are good reasons for thinking that our
Matthew may have been the last composed of the Synoptic
Gospels, and if so, it is obviously possible that the Markan
document may have come to the hands of the writer of
it with additions which it had not received when it lay

[1] See p. 122.

before St. Luke.' With this we would agree, only we hold that the subsequent additions were made by the hand of Mark himself, with still further additions in the third edition which is our canonical Mark.

We have dwelt at this length here on the question of the Markan document lying before the first and third evangelists because not only does a clearing up of this matter help us in deciding as to the exact contents of the Markan document, but it also has a distinct bearing upon the character and contents of the second document which has by common consent been designated ' Q.' For where we have matter common to the first and third Gospels, yet wanting in whole or in part from the second, its appearance in Matthew and Luke is often accounted for on the supposition that it was derived from Q. It will be shown that many of such instances are fully accounted for on the supposition that while they appeared in proto- and deutero-Mark, for some reason or other they were omitted, or considerably curtailed, when St. Mark came to draw up his latest edition, and in many cases it is not at all impossible to see the reasons which may have led him to make the alteration.

Early in 1911 there appeared a volume entitled *Oxford Studies in the Synoptic Problem*. This volume is the work of several members of the University of Oxford under the general editorship of Dr. Sanday. The members contributing, in addition to the editor, are Sir J. C. Hawkins, Archdeacon W. C. Allen, Dr. J. V. Bartlet, and the Revs. B. H. Streeter, W. E. Addis, and N. P. Williams. With such a composite authorship the book exhibits a certain amount of dissentient opinion between the different writers. Dr. Sanday minimises this difference of opinion, but to us it seems to be considerable. Thus Dr. Bartlet, and to some extent Archdeacon Allen, rejects the ' two-document theory,' while the others accept it. Sir J. C. Hawkins, in discussing the use of Q by the first and third

evangelists, considers that St. Luke did not use the same
collection of sayings as was used by St. Matthew.   Mr.
Streeter, on the other hand, considers that he did, and
that he has preserved the original order of Q better than
St. Matthew has done.   Dr. Allen again considers that the
first Gospel is the best authority for the contents of Q.
Dr. Bartlet, who contributes what he calls ' a Minority
Report,' accepting a two-document basis for the third
Gospel alone, holds that the special source of Luke was
bound up with Q and can scarcely be separated from it.
It is therefore far from easy to indicate the general opinion
of this school of criticism as a whole on the subject.

We notice a general abandonment of an oral basis for
the three Gospels.   The priority of Mark is allowed, but
in every case this priority is qualified.   The phrase
generally used is : ' What was practically identical with
Mark.'   But it may be asked, Wherein lay the difference
if there was not complete identity ?   It will be the purpose
of the following chapters to show that a thorough application of the theory of a proto-, deutero-, and trito-Mark
to documents will answer this and many other questions.
In considering the question whether Q contained narrative
as well as ' sayings ' properly so called, there seems to be
a general abandonment of Lightfoot's well-known contention that the term ' logion ' [1] might be used of scripture
generally without insisting too rigorously upon the meaning ' discourse.'   Yet the stories of the Baptism and the
Temptation, as well as that of the healing of the centurion's
servant, are all attributed to Q, in spite of the fact that in
the first Gospel the formula which always marks the
transition from discourse to narrative is used in passing
from the Sermon on the Mount to the healing of the
servant.   Apparently the inclusion of the three sections
in Q is due to the difficulty of accounting for the differences
between them as they appear in canonical Mark and as

[1] See p. 43.

they appear in the other two Gospels, supposing that canonical Mark was before the other evangelists. This question of the exact contents of the Markan source must be settled before we can hope to arrive at a conclusion as to the nature and composition of Q.

If it is at all possible to summarise criticism in England of the origins of the Synoptic Gospels, we may say that the general opinion, with notable exceptions, is as follows :—

1. The basis was documentary rather than oral.

2. The documents were two in number, and consisted of a collection or collections of ' sayings,' and a narrative portion corresponding most closely to canonical Mark.

3. In addition to these there were special sources available to the first and third evangelists which account for such features in both as the genealogical tables, the Messianic texts, and ' the Travel Document,' or Perean Section.

In America a notable contribution to the study of the Synoptic Problem is to be found in an able Introduction to a Commentary on the second Gospel by Dr. B. W. Bacon of Yale University. Dr. Bacon's conclusions are to the effect that the second Gospel is the work of a redactor, and very much more than a mere editing of St. Peter's discourses, inasmuch as it contains sections which show no intrinsic evidence of proceeding from such a source, and is dominated by theoretical considerations, often manifestly derived from the Pauline Epistles, especially Romans. He also holds that this redactor used Q to embellish and supplement an earlier and simpler Petrine narrative. Dr. Bacon does not discuss in detail the other sources, but he apparently holds that Q contained the sections which describe the preaching of the Baptist and the Baptism and Temptation of our Lord, and also that some

of the narrative supplements of Mark are derived from the
Lukan form of Q.

A more detailed and comprehensive discussion of the
whole question is to be found in an excellent reprint from
the Decennial Publications of the University of Chicago by
Dr. E. De Witt Burton, entitled *The Principles of Literary
Criticism and the Synoptic Problem.* We cannot do more
than summarise the conclusions of Dr. Burton, which are
as follows :—

1. Our Mark, or a document in large part identical with
   it, was employed as a source of both our first and
   third Gospels.
2. The Matthaean sources in addition to Mark are, a
   document not employed by Luke, made up chiefly
   or wholly of discourses and presumably the Logia
   of St. Matthew. In addition, two documentary
   sources common to Luke and Matthew are found
   in what are described as the Galilean document
   and the Perean document. Minor sources also
   exist in the infancy narrative, etc.
3. St. Luke has the same chief sources as are indicated
   in Matthew, with the exception of the Matthaean
   Logia as above said. He has interpolated material
   from the Galilean document into the Markan
   narrative, omitting St. Mark's similar narratives
   when they seemed to him less full and vivid, and
   adding the Perean document in two solid sections.
   The agreements of Matthew and Luke against
   Mark are left as an unexplained remainder by
   Dr. Burton.

It will thus be seen that the general results of criticism
in America are much the same as we have found in
England. Such differences as exist are prominent when
an effort is made to define more closely the sources of
the Gospels as we have them.

CHAPTER III

THE SAYINGS OF JESUS

THESE 'Sayings' constitute a prominent feature of the first and third Gospels. They are generally described as the non-Markan element in those Gospels, but the phrase is not sufficiently definitive. In the first place, it is still a moot question whether St. Mark does not, to some extent at least, introduce into the Gospel which bears his name sayings of our Lord technically so called. If he did, he may have drawn them from a source open to either or both of the other two evangelists. If again he did not, the phrase needs some further definition, inasmuch as matter may be Markan in origin, even though it do not appear in the second Gospel. Harnack seems to adopt the idea of a non-Markan element common to the first and third Gospels as indicating a certain source which was used by the evangelists of those Gospels, but, as Dr. Willoughby Charles Allen points out, the method is open to serious question ; for even if those two evangelists agree closely in many sections, it does not follow that they derived them from a single source. It will later on be shown that while the fact that the sayings in question are spoken by one teacher gives them a considerable amount of resemblance, there is nevertheless good reason for believing that the two evangelists derived them from different sources. Another descriptive title, used formerly in speaking of this source, is the word ' Logia.' But this again is open to misconception. For the same word seems to be used, notably in Romans iii. 2, where we should use the word ' Scriptures.' Such a term then might denote a docu-

ment which contained as much narrative as discourse, or
it might be used in a more strictly etymological sense to
describe more oracular sayings. The uncertainty would
then arise whether, when the word was used by any particular scholar, it was taken to cover a source consisting
entirely of sayings, or whether it connoted one which
contained a certain amount of historical matter, or in
other words a ' Gospel,' as the word is understood in our
days.

To avoid such difficulties the non-committal formula
' Q ' (=Quelle=Source) has found general acceptance of
late years. But, unfortunately, the uncertainty still
remains. We are told that St. Matthew caused to be
collected (συνετάξατο) the ' sayings ' (Logia) of Jesus.
Are we to suppose that this collection of St. Matthew's is
what we are to understand by Q ? Or does the formula
indicate some underlying basis of that apostle's work ?
Even then the question remains, and there seems no
probability of any immediate consensus of opinion on the
part of scholars, whether Q consisted entirely of discourse
or whether it contained—be it St. Matthew's work or not—
some admixture of narrative. If some agreement on
terms could be arrived at by scholars, the Synoptic
Problem would come appreciably nearer solution.

Collections of precepts spoken by their Master would
commend themselves very early to the disciples. The
treasuring up of sayings uttered by Rabbis was already a
common habit among the Jews, and that the followers of
Jesus should do the same was but natural under any
circumstances. But there was a certain character about
the sayings of Jesus which made them specially likely to
be early thrown together into some sort of collection.
They were terse, pointed, epigrammatic apophthegms
which could easily be retained in the memory. They
were didactic rather than historical, inasmuch as they
dealt with universal truths, and had a distinctly moral

and spiritual application. They might be expanded into
what we call a ' parable,' but the unity of the parable was
always some central truth, to which all other details were
but setting and scenery. Many of the most striking
of the sayings were in fact interpretations of the Mosaic
Law, which sounded a note far deeper and truer than
those to which the Jews had become accustomed in
Rabbinical schools. When the earliest Christians assembled
together to partake of the Agape, we may feel quite sure
that the sayings of the Master would form the text of many
a discourse, or they might be committed to memory in
the catechetical schools which were early established. In
the course of time a considerable number of these sayings
would be in vogue, and the collections would be continually
growing, as devout men and women called to remembrance
sayings which their Master had uttered. In such a method
of compilation there was room for a certain amount of
variety in the form in which the sayings were recorded.
Some memories would be more accurate than others, and
while the general idea was the same, there would be a
difference of expression when the same saying was given
by this one and by that. It was also inevitable that a
piety which was more imaginative than accurate would
put forth as sayings thoughts which belonged to their own
minds, and had never been spoken by Christ at all, and a
considerable number of spurious sayings would come into
existence in this way. If the question be asked how it is
that no such collection has survived, the answer would
probably be found to lie in the fact that such collections
were unauthorised, arbitrary, and exposed to the uncertainties attending such collections. A study of the
sayings which are to be found in the apocryphal Gospels
reveals many which it is difficult to accept as having been
spoken by our Lord. One such may be cited. It is
quoted by Origen from the Gospel according to the Hebrews.
' The Saviour Himself says : " Just now the Holy Spirit

my Mother, took me by one of my hairs, and carried me
away to the great mountain Tabor " ' (Origen, *In Johann.*
ii. 6). The gulf between such a saying and those which
appear in the Sermon on the Mount is immeasurable.
At the same time we may feel quite sure that the necessity
would be quickly felt of sifting this increasing quantity
of puerile and unworthy sayings, and the task of doing
this seems to have fallen in the first instance to St.
Matthew. Later on another attempt was made by St.
Luke, or by some unknown compiler whose work St. Luke
adopted, and as soon as these ' Authorised Versions,' as
we may call them, came into existence, their obvious
superiority would quickly lead to the disappearance of
inferior collections.

It is necessary to repeat here the often quoted passage
from Eusebius in which this work of St. Matthew's is
described. It is given as a statement made by Papias,
and occurs in the *Ecclesiastical History* (iii. 39). ' So then
Matthew composed the Logia in the Hebrew language,
and each one interpreted them as he was able.' It is to
be noted that in this passage we have a variant reading ;
the word συνεγράψατο = ' caused to be written ' appearing
in some MSS. instead of συνετάξατο ' caused to be drawn
up.' Dr. Arthur Wright prefers the reading συνετάξατο
as fitting in better with the idea of an oral basis for this
source. But even if συνετάξατο be preferred, it is difficult
to see how a definite compilation could be secured unless
the sayings were given in writing. Another indirect
allusion to the same work seems to be given by Papias
when, referring to St. Mark's memoirs of St. Peter's preaching, he says that Peter adapted his instructions to the
needs of his hearers, but had no design of giving ' a connected account of the Lord's Logia.' [1] Here, presumably,
we are led to infer that the ellipse may be supplied, ' as
St. Matthew had done.' It is to be noticed again that in

---

[1] σύνταξιν, cf. συνετάξατο in the former quotation.

this passage too there is a variant reading, some MSS.
giving λόγων instead of λογίων.

In considering these references to the work of St.
Matthew, we notice—

1. That it was originally written in Aramaic. This is
   borne out by other statements made both by
   Origen and Irenaeus. It follows from this that if
   the first Gospel contains St. Matthew's contribution
   to the Gospel story, it had been translated into
   Greek before it was added to the Markan narrative
   which the first Gospel undoubtedly contains.

2. St. Matthew's work was not a mere collection or
   accumulation of sayings. There was some method
   and plan in the matter. He arranged the sayings.
   The word συνετάξατο seems to indicate some
   classification or distribution of the sayings, and
   a more or less topical arrangement is at once
   suggested.

3. The phrase 'each one interpreted them as he was
   able' points to the use of these sayings in the
   assemblies of the Christian congregations, as we
   have already suggested. They formed exegetical
   material for moral and spiritual exhortations in
   the earliest Church, as they still do in the later
   Church of our own times.

Now when we turn from these Patristic references to
the Gospel itself we are at once struck with the fact that it
contains a considerable number of sections which come
under the description of such a word as Logia, if we
interpret that word in the sense of an utterance more or
less of an oracular character. These sections are sharply,
it will be seen that they are almost mechanically, divided
from the Markan narrative in which they are inserted.
Many of them are terse and epigrammatic, admirably constructed for remaining in the memory of those who listened

to them. Others are more in the character of a discourse,
while others again take the form of a parable. All, however, either enunciate or interpret great spiritual or moral
laws. They deal with what is universal rather than local,
and have to do with the inner spirit rather than the out-
ward expression of religious thought. The question has
never been fully discussed whether these sayings as they
exist in the first Gospel constitute the work of St. Matthew
as described by Papias. Most scholars content themselves with saying that the Logia of that apostle are lost,
and that these sections of the first Gospel are derived from
Q. With reference to this source again there is the greatest
uncertainty. Some hold that while it consisted for the
most part of discourses, it nevertheless contained a certain
amount of narrative. Even here there is uncertainty, for
some would assign to it a Passion narrative. Others,
like Harnack, cannot agree that it contained an account of
our Lord's Passion and Resurrection, and yet they assign
to it an account of the ministry of the Baptist, and the
story of our Lord's Temptation, and even an account
of the healing of the Centurion's servant. Dr. Allen very
pertinently asks what an account of the preaching of the
Baptist, or of the healing of the Centurion's servant, has
to do in a collection of discourses. Harnack points out
that while much attention has been given to the Markan
element in the Gospels, comparatively little has been
directed towards a definition of Q. A definition of this
source he himself attempts in a work, to which frequent
reference will be made by the present writer, but by
assuming that Q consists of the whole of the non-Markan
element in the first and third Gospels, and by the further
assumption (implied by the use of the same formula to
denote the source of both) that their authors used a common
document, he does not really carry us very much further
towards a solution of the problem. The importance of the
problem, as well as its difficulty, can scarcely be over-

estimated. Its solution will affect even our conclusions
with regard to the Markan question, which Harnack says
has been treated with scientific thoroughness. For, at
present, sections of the first and third Gospels are assigned
to Q which may after all be found to belong to that form
of the Markan narrative which the evangelists who compiled those Gospels used. The question really turns upon
whether Q is to be considered to be one document common
to St. Matthew and St. Luke, and whether it is to be held
to contain narrative as well as discourse. In approaching
this question the first thing to do is to attempt to come
to some decision with reference to the use of the word
λόγιον. Etymologically it would be most natural to take
it to denote something spoken, and as a diminutive of
λόγος it would stand for some brief utterance as distinguished from a lengthy or reasoned statement. As
such it was used to describe the utterances associated
with oracular shrines such as that at Delphi, and if the
use of the word could be thus limited we should have
no difficulty in coming to a conclusion. In 1875 Dr.
Lightfoot published his *Essays on Supernatural Religion*,
and in these the student will find a discussion of the use
of this word marked by the scholarship and research
which we generally associate with Lightfoot's name. In
this he contends that though the word was used to describe
'oracles,' properly so called, yet from the time of Philo
onwards it was used to cover a much wider connotation,
and that it was used by Philo and others in the sense in
which we use the word 'Scripture,' denoting thereby both
historical incident and didactic matter. It is certainly
so used by St. Paul in Romans iii. 2. But while we shall
agree that this use of the word was not uncommon in the
time when Papias wrote, he may quite well have used it
in the equally well-known sense of 'oracle.' In the writings
of Clement of Rome the word is used together with γραφαί,
as though that writer, in order that he might give a more

comprehensive expression covering both history and
discourse, used both the terms side by side. Lightfoot's
contention is well discussed by Sir John Hawkins
(*Ox. St.*, p. 105), and his conclusion is as follows : ' I think
that if a person who has freed himself, as it is not difficult
to do now, from all bias on either side, will take concord-
ances and indexes and will examine for himself the forty-
six places in which λόγιον occurs in the LXX or in the
Hexaplaric fragments, the four places in the New Testament,
the five places in Clement (Rom. i. and ii.) and Polycarp,
and the two in Justin Martyr, he will come to the conclusion
that the sense which a Christian writer of the date of
Papias would (apart from any special reason to the
contrary) naturally attach to the word is that of a divine
or sacred utterance. And this seems to be an opinion
widely and increasingly held by recent English writers.'
To the present writer this conclusion seems inevitable ;
and I shall therefore assume that if we are to seek for the
Matthaean contribution in the first Gospel, we must look
for ' sayings ' properly so called, and where we find words
of Jesus which occur in describing some incident in His
ministry they must be held over for the time as not belonging to the Matthaean part of the Gospel, until we are able
to assign them to some other of the different elements
which go to make up the first Gospel.

If sayings of our Lord were from an early date recited
and expounded in the Church, and afterwards collected
and written down, it is inevitable that the question should
arise whether indications of such sayings are to be found
elsewhere than in the two Gospels in which they appear
so conspicuously. The answer is distinctly affirmative.
There are traces of such both in the canonical writings of
the New Testament and in the writings that belong to
the sub-apostolic period of Church history, and the evidence
which these afford has been greatly strengthened by recent
discoveries in Egypt. If we could put ourselves in the

place of those for whom the New Testament writings
were first prepared, we should doubtless find that many
of the moral or spiritual exhortations contained in the
Epistles were the more pointed and authoritative, because
they were at once recognised as echoes of familiar words
spoken first by Him who remained the great Master of
Assemblies. Thus St. Paul in writing to the Corinthian
Church impresses upon them the importance of celebrating
the Lord's Supper, and in doing so uses words which are
not found in the institution of that Supper as recorded
in the Gospels, though a suggestion of them occurs in the
account given by St. Luke. 'As often,' he writes, 'as
ye eat this bread, and drink this cup, ye proclaim the
Lord's death until He come.' Now these words are given
in the *Apostolic Constitutions* as words of Christ Himself,
and the phraseology is identical with that which appears
in the Epistle to the Corinthians. They also appear as
distinct words of Jesus in several ancient liturgies, and it
thus seems probable that St. Paul uses these words as
conveying an injunction, already familiar to those to
whom he wrote, and authoritative, as being recorded
words of Christ Himself. There are many other moral
injunctions in the Epistles which are given as words of
Christ in non-canonical writings, but it seems uncertain
whether in the latter they are cited as the words of the
Lord because they occur in the Scriptures. It is possible
that they are repetitions of the Pauline injunction rather
than taken from some source common to St. Paul and to
the Father who uses them. We are on much surer
ground when we turn to the well-known passage in Acts
xx. 35 where St. Paul is represented as bidding the
Ephesian elders 'remember the words of the Lord Jesus,
how He Himself (αὐτός) said, "It is more blessed to give
than to receive."' These words occur in no edition of the
Gospels. They are quoted by Epiphanius (*Haer.* 74. 5),
and they also appear in the *Constitutions*. There can be

no reasonable doubt that they are a genuine Logion of Jesus, and their use by St. Paul offers presumptive evidence that he may have used others, even though he did not specifically declare their origin as in this case. Another likely saying given by St. Paul occurs in Ephesians iv. 26 : ' Let not the sun go down upon your wrath.' It is true that St. Paul does not ascribe the words to Jesus, but the somewhat formal way in which Origen does so in his Dialogue (*De recta Fide*), ' The Lord, being good, says, " The sun, let it not go down upon your wrath," indicates that he at any rate considered the words to have been spoken by Jesus.

Another passage generally accepted as an unrecorded ' saying ' is given by St. James where he speaks (i. 12) of ' the crown of life which the Lord hath promised to them that love Him.' No such ' saying ' occurs in the Gospels, but the phrase ' the crown of life ' occurs in Rev. ii. 10, and the use of the definite article, both here and in the Epistle of St. James, suggests that the phrase had become familiar in the Christian Church, and that the promise possessed a sanction which could only have been derived from Christ. There are other injunctions in the Epistle of St. James as there are in St. Paul's writings which read like ' sayings ' woven into the exhortations of the writer, but it is unnecessary to refer to any except those that can fairly be claimed as examples of unrecorded ' sayings,' and a single instance is enough for our present contention that such ' sayings ' were used in the early Church.

A striking and often quoted Logion is found in the great Cambridge Codex known by the name of *Codex Bezae*. In the sixth chapter of St. Luke's Gospel, where our Lord is represented as in controversy with the Pharisees on the subject of the keeping of the Sabbath, the following words occur : ' On the same day, seeing a man working on the Sabbath, He said to him, O man, if thou knowest what thou doest, blessed art thou ; but if thou knowest

not, thou art accursed and a transgressor of the law.'
The saying is one of extraordinary force, and is a distinct
echo of such teaching as our Lord is said to have given in
such passages as Matthew xii. 12, in which He shows that
there were certain works which might be done with
deliberation on the Sabbath day. It upholds the spirit
of the law, while it shows a proper reverence for that well-
being of mankind which our Lord maintains is the true
purpose of the law of the Sabbath when He says 'the
Sabbath was made for man.' The passage in *Codex
Bezae* is one of the many interpolations familiar in the
so-called Western Text. We cannot accept it as belonging
to St. Luke's original writing. It was probably inserted
at an early date, but its appearance again bears out our
contention that such sayings formed part of the treasured
inheritance of the early Church, and might or might not
be included in the canonical Gospels. We must content
ourselves with two instances from Patristic writings.
The former of them we take from Origen, who says in one
of his Homilies (*On Jerem.* xx. 3) : 'Moreover the Saviour
Himself says, He that is near Me is near the fire ; and he
who is far from Me, is far from the kingdom.' The saying
must be interpreted in very general terms to mean that
while the greater danger lay in being far removed from
Christ, yet proximity to Him who came to send fire upon
earth would mean a cleansing fire to one who, as St. Paul
said, built with wood, hay, or stubble. But whatever the
interpretation of this saying may be, there is no doubt
that Origen considered it to be a real saying of our Lord.
The second is also from Origen, though it is quoted by
several others of the Patristic writers. Origen says (*On
John,* xix. 2), 'The command of Jesus which says, Become
ye approved bankers.' In the *Pistis Sophia* also we read,
'The Saviour of Mary replies, "I said to you of old, Be
ye as prudent bankers, take the good, cast out the bad." '
And Chrysostom, after giving the Logion, says, 'Not that

ye should stand in the market-place and count silver coins, but that ye may test your words with all exactness' (*Chrysostom*, v. 844). The above may be taken as examples, which might be considerably augmented, of sayings which were attributed to our Lord, and it is to be noticed that they all possess the common characteristics of terse moral injunctions conveyed in such a way as to be easily carried in the memory. It may be said that there is a slight difference between these and those which appear in the Gospels, but this difference may be due to our familiarity with those that are extant in the Scriptures, and they certainly differ much more from the extravagant and puerile sayings often attributed to Christ in the Apocryphal Gospels. But whether they are genuine or not does not make much difference to our argument, which is that it was well known that from earliest times sayings of a certain character were attributed to our Lord, and that these were treasured in the memory of the faithful, and were freely quoted in homilies delivered to the Church.

These indications of the use of the Lord's sayings received additional significance by the discovery in 1897 of a leaf of papyrus containing eight sayings similar in character yet differing from those which were extant before. They were discovered by Messrs. Grenfell and Hunt in the village of Oxyrhynchus, south of Cairo, and were speedily given to the world in an edition in which the lacunæ, or gaps in the text caused by the breaking away of the papyrus, were tentatively filled up by capable scholars. The sayings have no sort of connection with one another ; each is entirely detached, and is introduced by the simple formula, ' Jesus saith.' No historical framework was considered necessary for the different sayings, each was recorded for its independent value, and the whole collection would probably be used for purposes of meditation by some early Christian. The sayings are as follows :—

1. Jesus saith, Except ye fast to the world, ye shall in

nowise find the kingdom of God ; and except ye make the Sabbath a real Sabbath, ye shall not see the Father.

2. Jesus saith, I stood in the midst of the world, and in the flesh was I seen of them ; and I found all men drunken, and none found I athirst among them. And my soul grieveth over the sons of men, because they are blind in their heart, and see not their wretchedness and their poverty.

3. Jesus saith, Wherever there are two, they are not without God ; and wherever there is one alone, I say I am with him. Raise the stone and there thou shalt find me ; cleave the wood and there am I.

4. Jesus saith, A prophet is not acceptable in his own country ; neither doth a physician work cures upon those who know him.

5. Jesus saith, A city built upon the top of a high hill, and established, cannot fall nor be hidden.

6. Jesus saith, Thou hearest with one ear (but the other thou hast closed).

7. . . . And then shalt thou see clearly to cast out the mote that is in thy brother's eye.

8. . . . Poverty. . . .

The editors of these striking sayings have put forward the following propositions :—

1. The sayings were part of a collection of sayings, not extracts from a Gospel.

2. They were independent of our Four Gospels in their present shape.

3. They were put together earlier than A.D. 140, and it might be in the first century.

4. They do not belong to heretical writings.

These propositions seem to have met with general acceptance, and there can be very little doubt that they form part of some collection loosely strung together for didactic or devotional purposes. Their independence of canonical Scripture is full of significance. The collector, whoever he was, had access to some other source than that which is furnished by our Gospels, and if there was one there may have been many in the earliest Church. They differ in tone and spirit from the great majority of those which appear in the Gospel according to the Hebrews, the Ebionite Gospel, and other apocryphal writings. Now as soon as we consider these sayings thus put together we are bound to recall the statement made by Papias, and already quoted, as to a collection of the sayings of our Lord which Matthew made in the Hebrew tongue, and on which Papias himself is said to have written a commentary. The question arises whether that collection of St. Matthew's could have been anything of this sort. If the phraseology of Papias, as quoted by Eusebius, can be relied upon, the answer must be in the negative. For the word $\sigma\acute{v}\nu\tau\alpha\xi\iota\varsigma$ indicates some sort of arrangement, and not a mere accumulation of disjointed utterances such as we have here. It will be further shown that we have in the first Gospel something which comes much nearer to the description of St. Matthew's work which Papias gives us.

When we turn from these ' sayings ' to those which are recorded in the first and third Gospels, we see that the latter can be placed under two categories. We have sayings which spring out of some incident, and the narration of the incident is necessary for discovering the point of the saying. The words spoken by Christ, for instance, in connection with His temptation, require what we may call the historical setting before they become intelligible to us ; and when He says of the Centurion ' I have not found so great faith, no, not in Israel,' the statement is without point unless we read it in connection with the request of the Centurion. Such sayings, too, lack

the ' oracular ' character which others reveal. They deal
with special instances rather than with universal truths.
We have urged elsewhere, in connection with the supposed
use of Q by St. Mark, that the appearance of words spoken
by our Lord when performing a miracle, or when dealing
with those who sought Him, does not necessarily imply
derivation from a collection of sayings properly so called,
and the Synoptic Problem will have come appreciably
nearer solution if scholars can agree to distinguish between
statements of our Lord made in the course of His common
intercourse with men, and those which He made when He
dealt with great underlying principles of life and godliness.
These last belong to the second of our two categories.
They resemble in form and structure those which we have
discovered in the Epistles and in extra-canonical writings,
and there is a strong likeness between them and those
discovered at Oxyrhynchus. They are independent of
any setting of narrative or historical statement. Any of
them may quite well be found in a catalogue of apophthegms
needing no other introduction than that which has now
become familiar—' Jesus saith.' Sayings that belong to
the former class may then be accounted for in connection
with some narrative source, and we may consider with
reference to the second whether or no there are indications
of some collection or collections of ' oracles ' that will
account for those features of both the first and third
Gospels which differentiate them from the second. If it
be possible to account for the former class as belonging
to a narrative source, then the term Q could be used for
the second, and if this could become the universal custom
of scholars the gain would be very great, for, as we have
shown, there is no common use of terms at present, and
' Q ' seems to represent some sort of receptacle to which
are relegated all the bits and ends of Gospel sections, the
origin of which seems to be uncertain. Dr. Burkitt
contends that Q was a Gospel now irretrievably lost, but

the present writer holds that there is far more to be said
for Dr. Sanday when he writes :—

' The leading purpose of this little book appears to have
been to set before its readers some account of the Christian
ideal, the character and mode of life expected of them as
Christians. It was felt that this could best be done by
collecting together a number of typical sayings and discourses of Christ. There was no idea of writing a biography,
and not even in this case of composing a ' gospel ' (or full
statement of the redeeming acts of Christ), but only a
brief exemplar to set before the eyes and minds of converts' (*Encyclopædia of Religion and Ethics*, vol i. p. 575).

Harnack also does not allow that Q contained a Passion
narrative, and states that it was no Gospel like Matthew,
Mark, and Luke, though it was not a mere formless compilation of sayings and discourses without any thread of
connection. He does, however, allow that it contained
the story of the baptism of Jesus with its closely connected
sequel, the temptation, and adds to these the account of
the healing of the Centurion's servant. Dr. Stanton is in
general agreement with this. If these scholars could see
their way to remove from Q the narratives above
mentioned, as they have already removed the story of the
Passion, the question of these sources would be immensely
simplified, and, as it seems to me, a fair solution of a
difficult problem would come at last into sight.

It is not difficult to see why it is found convenient to
relegate the stories of the baptism, the temptation, and the
healing of the Centurion's servant to Q. It is because of
the great difficulty of accounting for these as coming from
the Markan source, always supposing that by ' the Markan
source ' we are to understand canonical Mark. The last
of the three is not given at all by St. Mark in the second
Gospel, and his account of the baptism and temptation
is so exceedingly brief, as compared with the other accounts,
that it is impossible to suppose that the editors of the first

and third Gospels took the liberty of amplifying to the
extent which they must have done if only canonical Mark
was before them. It is thought better to refuse a Markan
origin for these sections, and if we ask where then their
source is to be found, the answer is ' in Q.' I would urge
that this avoidance of one difficulty only leads us to another.
It is exceedingly difficult to see what an account of the
Baptist's ministry has to do with sayings and discourses
of Christ. Our Lord's words in reply to the Tempter differ
in essential characteristics from the sayings which we have
in the Sermon on the Mount ; and, as we have already
seen, to claim that the word ' I have not found so great
faith, no, not in Israel,' belongs to a collection of ' sayings,'
is criticism in despair. There is another and a better way
out of this difficulty, It is to accept, what I hope to show
has very much in its favour, that St. Mark wrote down his
memoirs of St. Peter's preaching more than once, and that
in earlier editions, prepared one in Palestine and the other
in the interests of a Jewish-Christian community, a full
account of the Baptist's ministry, and of his relation to
our Lord, would be entirely in place ; these subjects,
however, would be mentioned in the briefest possible way
in a later edition prepared in Rome, for a Church which
was largely Gentile. These earlier editions would
naturally include also the account of the coming of the
Centurion, because the point of our Lord's words on that
occasion was that Israel had failed to evince the faith
which He had found in this Gentile.

We may account for the inclusion of a Passion narrative
in Q by some scholars, though not by any means by all,
in the same way. When we make a comparative study of
the three accounts of our Lord's Passion, we find that the
first and second Gospels are in close correspondence, but
St. Luke obviously departs to a considerable extent from
them, and he departs entirely in his account of the resurrection appearances of our Lord. The question then

arises : if he did not derive this matter from St. Mark, from what source did he obtain it ? Again the answer is ' from Q,' and so we are presented with the theory that this collection of sayings and discourses contained an account of the Passion. Then when arguments against this are brought forward, we have Dr. Burkitt rounding upon his critics and saying : ' I find it difficult to believe that a critical method is wholly to be trusted, which presents us with a document that starts off with the story of our Lord's Baptism, and then gives us His words but not the story of His Cross and Resurrection.' To my mind Dr. Burkitt is here (*Journ. of Theol. Stud.*, p. 454) unanswerable, but a truer conclusion than that which he gives us seems to be this—that neither the Baptism nor the Passion story belongs to Q ; that the one belongs to an earlier edition of St. Mark than that which we have in the second Gospel, and the other belongs to that special source which, as we shall show,[1] St. Luke so freely used. I would therefore strongly urge that the term Q be reserved for a collection of sayings properly so called, and that all sections which contain anything of narrative which is more than a mere introduction be assigned to some other source. Among such sections would certainly be found the three to which we have just referred.

But having got as far as this we are confronted by a further question. Are we to suppose that Q thus interpreted stands for the collection of our Lord's sayings which we learn from Papias St. Matthew compiled ? Or are we to use the term Q for some such collection as that of which we have a fragment remaining in the Oxyrhynchus Logia ? And what is St. Luke's relation to this collection ? Did he use the Matthaean collection ? Or did he use, as St. Matthew did, some collection of sayings which he reduced to some sort of order ? If the latter, was the collection before him the same as, or other than, that

[1] See chap. **vi**.

before St. Matthew ?   To these questions we must now
address ourselves.

If by Q we are to understand the Matthaean collection
of sayings, then it will follow that St. Luke used St.
Matthew in all that part of his Gospel which contains sayings
of Jesus, and against this, as we shall see, there are great
objections which may be brought whenever we say that
St. Luke derived this or that from Q. Further, if we identify
Q with the Matthaean collection, and if this—as Dr.
Burkitt and others maintain—is no longer extant, then it
is difficult to see why St. Matthew's name ever came to be
connected with the first Gospel.   The Logian sections of
the first Gospel would in that case be a mere selection
from the work of that apostle.   His connection with the
book would be considerably more remote.   But if we
present ourselves with the hypothesis that St. Matthew
had before him one of the many loose and informal collections of sayings of which the Oxyrhynchus papyrus
is a type, and if he distributed these sayings which he could
accept as genuine under different heads, making his distribution topical in its scheme ; if further this σύνταξις,
so far from being lost, actually exists in the first Gospel,
sandwiched between blocks of Markan narrative, we shall
at once account for the statements of Papias, and also for
the association of St. Matthew's name with the first
Gospel.   Before such a hypothesis can be accepted it must
of course be tested in the light of what is given us in the
first Gospel.   This part of our task will be attempted in
the chapter in which we discuss that Gospel more in detail,
but for the sake of clearness I would here reconstruct the
history of the production of the first Gospel somewhat
as follows.

The words of the Lord Jesus began to be quoted and
expounded in the Christian assemblies at a very early date.
To facilitate such work, and also for the purpose of private
meditation on the part of individual Christians, collections

of such sayings began to appear. These were in no sort of
order, nor was it necessary to do more by way of introducing them than to use the formula ' Jesus saith.' But
the method was open to abuse. The sayings could not
always be guaranteed, and spurious sayings began to be
attributed to our Lord. St. Matthew then undertook the
task of drawing up a collection of true sayings, and he
did so in their original Aramaic, each speaker in the
Christian assemblies translating or expanding them as he
was able. In this way full justice is done to the statement
of Papias which Eusebius records. But when Hellenistic
Jews began to enter the Christian Church, the Aramaic,
in which the sayings were recorded, was felt to be a
difficulty, and at a comparatively early date the sayings
were translated into Greek. In this form they found their
way to some centre in which there were a number of Jewish
Christians. The conditions of a Church in Alexandria
would exactly correspond with the imaginary conditions
which we have thus laid down. But that Church had
other treasures than this collection of sayings. St. Mark
had been one of its first ' bishops,' and he had even before
coming to Egypt drawn up some memoirs of St. Peter's
preaching. That he would do so again for the Church in
Egypt we may feel assured, and for some time the two
documents would exist side by side. The arrangement,
however, was awkward, and later on an attempt was made
to join the two documents, and at the same time to add
other matter which had come to hand. This was done in
the simplest way by introducing the different Matthaean
sections bodily into the Markan narrative, at such points
as seemed suitable, and a simple formula was used to form
such connections as were felt to be necessary to make a
single volume out of the two.

When we turn from the first Gospel to the third we
notice at once that whether St. Luke used the same source
as St. Matthew did or not, he has undoubtedly distributed

his material on a different principle. St. Matthew has arranged his sayings topically, bringing together in five sections (though some critics consider the number to be seven and others eight) what he considered represented the teaching of Jesus, each section having a theme of its own. These five sections are discussed in the chapter which deals with the first Gospel. St. Luke, however, arranged his Logian material not topically but chronologically, distributing them among the Markan and other sections which appear in his Gospel in such a way as to give the impression that they were spoken on certain occasions indicated by the evangelist. Thus, to take a well-known example, St. Matthew places the Lord's Prayer in the considerable body of sayings which he has put together and which we call ' the Sermon on the Mount.' St. Luke, however, shows us that the prayer was given by our Lord quite late in His ministry, on an occasion when His disciples approached Him with the request that He would teach them to pray.

It is generally accepted that St. Luke no less than St. Matthew used Q, and an attempt has been made to decide which of the two kept the closer to their common source, and from the conclusion arrived at it is generally thought that some guidance may be reached with a view to the reconstruction of Q. Thus Dr. Stanton says : ' If we ask in which of the two writers the contents of a document which both have used, or two editions of which they respectively used, is most likely to be given in its original order, there can be no question that it is in St. Luke.' Dr. Stanton is here in agreement with Dr. Burkitt, but it is to be noticed that both of these critics assume Q to be a document containing narrative as well as discourses, and this, as we have shown, is a point to be settled by discussion, and not assumed. If the source underlying the Logian sections of the two Gospels be, as we prefer to regard it, a collection of sayings without order or definite arrangement, or rather of two such collections, then it becomes unnecessary to discuss which of the two adheres the more closely to the original. Schmiedel seems to feel this uncertainty, for he contends that if we are to consider which of the two has preserved the Logia in the more original form, the answer must be that it is sometimes the one and sometimes the other. Dr. Plummer has pointed out in his commentary on the third Gospel that absence or scarcity of the characteristics of St. Luke is most common in the matter which appears in the first and third Gospels, and he infers from this that where the materials were already in Greek, St. Luke would use them without any great amount of alteration. 'It is incredible that two or three independent translations should agree almost word for word.' This, however, scarcely affects the conclusion at which we have arrived, that the Logia in the first Gospel came from a source other than that which was used by St. Luke, for none of the passages cited by Dr. Plummer in illustration are taken from the five great blocks of sayings which appear in the first Gospel. The fact that Lukan characteristics are most lacking in passages taken from Logian sections would indicate St. Luke's special reverence for this particular source, and if we find that there is any considerable difference between the sayings in the one Gospel and the sayings in the other, we may safely infer that St. Luke did not use the same collection as did St. Matthew. Now this is precisely what we do find. Dr. Stanton indeed points out that the degree of correspondence varies in the third Gospel, that in some passages the sayings are identical, and in others there is more difference. He would single out those sayings in which the correspondence is so close as to lead us to conclude that the two evangelists used a common source, and he would account for the sayings in which there is more difference by ascribing that difference to conditions affecting the translation into Greek of the Aramaic collection of sayings. But may not

the explanation be a far simpler one ?   If there were many
attempts to set forth the facts of our Lord's life and
teaching, we have only to suppose that one collection of
sayings was used by St. Matthew and another by St. Luke
to sufficiently account for the differences, while the
character of these sayings, their epigrammatic form, and
the reverence in which such sayings would be held, would
completely account for the fact that some sayings would
appear in the one collection in a form all but identical
with that in which they appear in the other.   The differences, moreover, are too great for us to account for them
merely on the score of translation.   The different versions
of the Beatitudes alone is sufficient to settle this.   We
may feel sure that in this section least of all would St.
Luke feel himself at liberty to amend the form in which
he found the sayings, yet his version differs considerably
from that in St. Matthew's Gospel.   In the section of St.
Luke which most corresponds with the ' Sermon,' as given
in the first Gospel, we are told that our Lord stood upon a
level place where St. Matthew speaks of ' the mountain.'
There is no necessary contradiction in this, but in the
sayings which follow our Lord is represented as speaking
directly to His disciples: ' Blessed are ye poor . . .
Blessed are ye that hunger,' etc., while in the first Gospel
the form is more general: ' Blessed are the poor,' etc.   The
number of Beatitudes is different.   There are only four in
Luke, while there are nine in the first Gospel.   In the third
Gospel the Beatitudes are followed by a corresponding
number of woes which do not appear in the first Gospel.
Again, the Beatitudes in the third Gospel are simpler in
form and more universal in application, while in the other
there is some amount of interpretation of the general
truth ; thus ' the poor ' in the one becomes ' the poor in
spirit ' in the other.   There is the same difference in the
saying in which ' salt ' is used to convey the teaching.   St.
Matthew gives us the Logion as follows : ' Ye are the salt

of the earth, but if the salt lose its savour wherewith shall it be salted ? It is good for nothing but to be cast out and trodden underfoot of men.' This appears in the third Gospel in quite another setting and in the following form : ' Salt is good, but if even the salt have lost its savour wherewith shall it be seasoned ? It is fit neither for the land nor for the dunghill ; men cast it out.'

Instances of such differences may easily be multiplied, but these will suffice to show the difficulty of believing that St. Luke used the same document as St. Matthew did. If the two evangelists had the same document or even two editions of the same document before them, one or the other must have allowed himself an amount of freedom in transcribing them of which we have no evidence elsewhere in their respective writings. Neither can we believe that St. Luke would have taken the liberty to separate and distribute the sayings as he has done, if they appeared in his source thrown together into the considerable ' blocks ' in which they appear in the first Gospel. Now all these difficulties disappear in a moment if we can accept the theory that the two evangelists had before them different collections of sayings thrown together without any attempt to arrange them under different heads, or to indicate the occasion on which each was spoken by Christ. The freedom in that case would be readily allowed them to arrange these as each thought best. St. Matthew preferred to bring together those which bore upon some aspect or other of ' the kingdom,' St. Luke attempted to place each in its chronological setting. The form of the saying will account for whatever likeness may be discovered between the two versions ; the more epigrammatic it was the more likely was it that it would be identical in the two versions. At the same time, the fact that it was written down by different persons in the first instance would account for whatever difference may appear between the two versions. The two sources, we are convinced, would resemble the collection discovered at Oxyrhynchus, and just as in that collection we have the saying, ' And then shalt thou see clearly to cast out the mote that is in thy brother's eye,' which has a great amount of resemblance to the corresponding logion in the first Gospel, and yet differs from it, so we may be sure, between those used by St. Luke and those used by St. Matthew, there would be likeness and unlikeness. They would be like in the essential teaching, and yet would vary in the form of expression.

We conclude then that if the formula Q be still used to indicate the logion source, it should be used to indicate a far more simple and elementary source than one which, by adding narrative to logia, would partake of the character of a Gospel, and in order to show that the source used by one evangelist differed from that used by the other, we should make the further differentiation of Q (L) and Q (M).

CHAPTER IV

THE FIRST GOSPEL

In discussing the many questions which arise out of a study of the first Gospel we shall find ourselves obliged to repeat much that we have already stated in the preceding chapter, for the problem of the first Gospel is bound up in the problem of Q. In so far as the Markan element in it is concerned, critics have arrived at a fair amount of agreement. Zahn is now the only critic of eminence who maintains that the first Gospel was prior to the second, and was used by St. Mark. He does so largely upon the consideration that the evidence from Papias points to a Hebrew Gospel prepared by St. Matthew, and this Hebrew original, he maintains, was afterwards translated by St. Mark into Greek. He thus accounts in part, but not entirely, for differences between the first and second Gospel on the ground of translation. The second of the two great arguments he brings forward refers to the character of the contents of the first Gospel. These show that it must have been written for Jewish Christians, and therefore it could scarcely be dependent upon a work written at Rome and for Gentiles. He also considers that in Matthew ' the material stifles the thought. On the other hand, in spite of numerous infelicities of expression, Mark shows himself a master in clear narrative, in his ability to portray a situation, and to reproduce with exactness trivial details, which in the memory of an eye-witness, are inseparably connected with the kernel of the event. If this is true it follows that Matthew is more original. It would be inconceivable that with the narratives of Mark before him, which for the most part are very clearly drawn and accurate in details, he should have obliterated or otherwise destroyed those characteristics without intending either to correct errors or to make considerable abridgment.' [1]

These contentions of Zahn have often been met and refuted. The student will find an admirable discussion of them in Dr. Stanton's work.[2] We shall not attempt to go over the same ground, but we would point out that Zahn's position is really based upon two assumptions each of which fails to commend itself. The former of the two is this, that by the Logia of St. Matthew written in Hebrew we are to understand the first Gospel as it stands in the Christian canon. A far better interpretation of the reference in Eusebius is that which considers that the term Logia is to be used not of a Gospel, but of a collection of sayings uttered by our Lord, preserved in the memory of the earliest Church, and thrown into form and order by St. Matthew.

The second assumption is that when we speak of the priority of Mark we are shut up to the idea of the priority of the canonical Gospel known by that name. If it can be shown that there is good reason to suppose that St. Mark wrote his Gospel more than once, and that it is an earlier edition which is contained in the first Gospel, an edition too which bears distinct signs, as Zahn declares, of having been prepared in the interests of Jewish Christians, then it follows that there may well be a Markan element in the first Gospel which will agree with the rest of that Gospel in exhibiting Jewish characteristics, and in maintaining a ' unity of design,' and that nevertheless in the later canonical Mark we shall have as distinct a Gentile reference and as great a richness of detail as that which Zahn, quite correctly, considers to belong to a late work.

Accepting then the idea of the priority of Mark as

---

[1] *Intro. to the New Test.*, (Eng. Trans.), vol. ii. p. 606.
[2] P. 38 ff.

established in this sense, we proceed to mark off three
main sections in the first Gospel. These are :

1. A Nativity section consisting of chapters i. and ii.
2. A Markan section which is not consecutive, but
   is arranged alternately with blocks of matter to
   which the description ' discourses ' may be assigned.
3. A section consisting of discourses. These are
   sandwiched between Markan sections, as we have
   said, and possess distinct characteristics of first-
   rate importance as indicating the origin and purpose
   of the Gospel.

In addition to these main divisions we notice that the
editor of the Gospel had before him a collection of
Messianic proof-texts, which he inserted in the record
wherever he thought it desirable to do so. These must
be distinguished from quotations from the Jewish
Scriptures made by our Lord Himself. They are easily
distinguished as belonging rather to the comment of the
evangelist than to Christ, and they are usually introduced
by the formula ' that it might be fulfilled,' ἵνα πληρωθῇ,
or its equivalent. They appear in the following passages :
i. 23, ii. 6, 15, 18, 23, iv. 14-16, viii. 17, xii. 17-21, xiii. 35,
xxi. 5, xxvii. 9-10. These citations greatly intensify the
strong Jewish point of view which Zahn and others discover in the Gospel, but they present no great difficulty
in connection with the Synoptic Problem. They are
clearly interpolations, taken from a variety of sources
some of which are not to be discovered in the Old
Testament.

The Nativity section stands alone. There are linguistic
peculiarities such as the use of ' behold,' ἰδοῦ, after a
genitive absolute which occur only in these chapters ; but
apart from these we have the story of the Massacre of the
Innocents and the flight into Egypt, of which we have
no mention in the Nativity section of the third Gospel.

Further, St. Luke places the home of the holy family in Nazareth, both before and after the birth of our Lord, while St. Matthew says that the home was in Bethlehem, and that after the flight into Egypt Joseph removed to Nazareth from fear of Archelaus. But above all, what makes the two accounts distinct is the fact that the one story is clearly that which would be given by Joseph, while that in St. Luke is as clearly that which could have been derived from Mary alone. The story of the birth of our Lord is preceded by a genealogical table, the purpose of which seems to be, as Zahn points out, not so much to give the Davidic descent of Jesus, as to show that the Jesus who received the name Messiah was ' the goal of the entire history of His people.' This is shown by the incompleteness of the table considered as a line of unbroken descent, and by an indication of ' the change brought about in the Davidic house when the unity of the family and the inheritance of the promise were no longer repre- sented in one person who occupied the throne, but when what was once the royal seed continued to exist only as a number of families, with uncertainty as to which one would enter upon the inheritance.' These characteristics of the section will have a strong determining influence when we come to consider the circumstances, local and temporal, in which this Gospel, as a whole, was produced, but they have little to do with the Synoptic Problem, which is mainly concerned with the inter-relations of the three Gospels. These come into view when we take account of the three main questions, which are :

1. To what extent does this Gospel depend upon Mark, and what is the relation of its Markan material to the corresponding portion of the third Gospel and also to canonical Mark ?

2. What is the Matthaean contribution which will

E

account for the traditional title given to this
Gospel ?

3. To what extent is it dependent upon another document (Q), and does it share this dependence with
   Luke ?

These three questions really overlap. It is scarcely
possible to discuss the Markan element without reference
to the Matthaean, for what cannot be assigned to the
one will generally find its place in the other, and as we
have seen, our definition of Q involves a definition of the
Matthaean Logia. It is the overlapping of these questions
which has made the question of Gospel Origins appear so
hopeless of solution to the general reader. To us the clue
out of the labyrinth is to be found in a phrase which
occurs five times, and always in passing from a section
containing discourse to narrative. That phrase occurs
first at the close of the Sermon on the Mount, where we
read (vii. 28), 'And it came to pass when Jesus had
ended these words the multitudes were astonished at His
teaching.' The same phrase, or a variant which is a
distinct equivalent, occurs also at xi. 1, xiii. 53, xix. 1, and
xxvi. 1. If we give our attention to what precedes we
shall find that in each case it consists of a number of
sayings many of them cast in the form of epigram, and
entirely independent of historical setting, others expanded
into parables, and others again taking the form of set
discourses, but all of them dealing with what we have
called ' universals,' or the great basal spiritual principles
which underlie our Lord's conception and teaching concerning the Kingdom of Heaven. In each case the section
which follows is distinctly Markan. It is found in both
the first and second Gospel, and the linguistic characteristics are very close. If, now, we remove these sections
which, whatever they may be, are certainly not Logian,
we find that we have five blocks of quite homogeneous

matter. They evidently belong to one source, and that source is other than the Markan Gospel, in whatever sense this last be interpreted.

Before we pass, however, to consider what that source can be, we ought to consider whether any other sections of the first Gospel belong to the same category, and four passages at once attract attention, inasmuch as they also contain a considerable amount of the teaching of our Lord, and also because they are not found in canonical Mark. These are, as a rule, referred by critics to Q, and the reference is due to two facts; first, they are words spoken by our Lord, which is supposed to stamp them as 'sayings,' and secondly, they are not found in canonical Mark, and for this reason are supposed to belong to a non-Markan source. But when we come to examine them we find that they possess certain features which differentiate them from the five blocks which we have now taken out of the first Gospel, and on the other hand, there are considerations which suggest a Markan source for the sections in spite of the fact that they do not occur in canonical Mark. The first section is that which is found in xi. 2-30. This consists of the account of the Baptist's message to Jesus, and of our Lord's vindication of His Fore-runner. To this must be added the section beginning at verse 20, which is closely connected with the preceding ('Then began Jesus to upbraid,' etc.). In idea also the latter follows on the Baptist section, inasmuch as the cities mentioned had not known the day of their visitation any more than those to whom the Baptist had made his appeal in vain. The section differs from the five blocks aforesaid because its historical setting is necessary before the point of the teaching can be apprehended. The reference is not universal, as is the case with the different parts of the Sermon on the Mount, but is circumscribed by the particular and local relations of the Baptist to the Jews on the one hand, and to Christ on the other. Another

significant fact is this, that it is to be found in the third
Gospel though not in the second.

Now when we come to consider the second Gospel we
shall at once be struck with the fact that its reference to
the ministry of the Baptist is extremely scanty as compared
with what we find in the other two Gospels. This is far
from indicating, in our opinion, that the account of the
Baptist's ministry in the first and third Gospels must be
referred to Q. To those who would so relate it, it is
sufficient to ask with Dr. Willoughby Allen what the
record of the Baptist's preaching has to do with a collection of the discourses of Jesus. A far better explanation of the fuller record of the Baptist's ministry in the
first and third Gospel is to be found in a distinction between
the Markan sections of those Gospels and canonical Mark.
As soon as we have grasped the fact, as it seems to me,
that the Markan element in the first and third Gospels
was in each case earlier than canonical Mark, and that
they were written in Palestine in the one case and for
Jewish Christians in the other, while the second Gospel,
as we have it, was written for Gentiles in Rome and considerably later, then we see that references in the first
and third to the Baptist were likely to be full. Their
interest would be great and immediate, while in Rome they
would be remote and comparatively unimportant. Thus
the section xi. 2-30 would belong, like the fuller account
of the baptism and temptation of our Lord, to the earlier
editions of the Markan narrative, though it does not
appear in canonical Mark. There is no apparent reason
why it should be considered to have come from the same
source as the Sermon on the Mount.

The second passage of the class now under consideration
consists of the first sixteen verses of the twentieth chapter.
The parable of the labourers in the vineyard does not
occur in either of the other two Gospels. Now if this
parable belongs to Q, we may well ask for what reason St.

Luke omitted it from his Gospel. The teaching it contains was admirably suited to one who held with St. Paul that though the Gentiles might enter the kingdom later than did the Jews, they were nevertheless equal in privilege, and fellow-heirs of the grace of God. It is one of the parables which, we consider, St. Luke would have made haste to transcribe if he had found it in Q. But the question remains whether it did belong to Q. It is closely connected, both grammatically and logically, with the section which precedes. St. Peter had said to his Master, ' Lo, we have left all and followed Thee ; what shall we have therefore ? ' The thought of rewards was distinctly before him. Christ closes His reply with the words, ' Many that are first shall be last, and the last first,' and then follows the parable ' *For* the kingdom of heaven is like. . . .' To us it seems that St. Luke does not record the saying because it never was in his source. It belongs to the deutero-Mark, and may with confidence be included in the Markan section of the first Gospel.

Another similar passage is that in which we have the parable of the royal marriage feast (Matt. xxii. 1-14). This passage, too, does not occur in the second Gospel, and those who refer everything that does not so occur to Q have no hesitation in ascribing the parable to that source. Unlike the preceding parable in chapter xxi. this is found in the third Gospel ; but there it appears not in those sections in which St. Luke appears to be using a collection of sayings, but in that part of the third Gospel which is known by the name of ' the Travel Document,' and which is peculiar to that Gospel. It is given by St. Luke in chapter xiv. 15-24, and if the passage is compared with its equivalent in the first Gospel, it will be seen how different it is in wording and detail. Now we have already seen that the characteristics of St. Luke are least frequent in those passages in which he uses his collection of sayings. He seems least willing to make

changes when he is dealing with the words of Jesus, and
if the difference is to be explained on the ground of editorial
privilege, it must be admitted that here the third evangelist
departs from his usual practice. Is it at all necessary for
us to do so ? It follows a section in the first Gospel which
is distinctly Markan, and its main purpose is closely
connected with what precedes, for in each we have the
neglect and insult of the lord which culminates in the
murder of his servants. In each the lord punishes his
rebellious subordinates with death, and their privilege
is given to others. The section is so closely connected
with what we have in Mark that it seems better to assign
this passage too to the Markan source, and the fact
that it does not appear in the second Gospel presents no
difficulty to those who consider that the three Gospels
present us with three editions of Markan writing. The
custom of ascribing everything of a parabolic nature to
Q does not seem to us to be sound criticism. Indeed it is
impossible to eliminate from Mark all parabolic teaching.
As we have elsewhere shown, St. Mark does not use Q,
but there is no reason why in his writings the words and
parables of the Lord should not appear, as they certainly
do in chapter iv. We may be quite sure that though
St. Peter dealt for the most part with those works of
Christ which declared Him to be the Son of God, he would
not hesitate to give the teaching of our Lord if the occasion
seemed to him to demand it, and that Mark recorded this
parable in his second edition we have very little doubt. It
was spoken during our Lord's journey up to Jerusalem,
but there is little trace of chronological exactness in these
memoirs of St. Peter's preaching. St. Luke has given
the occasion of its utterance with greater accuracy, but
the details of the parable in the two records vary inasmuch
as it was derived from different sources.

The last of these passages is that which occurs in chapter
xxiii. 15-39. This again is closely connected with a

preceding Markan section though it does not appear in
canonical Mark. It is the passage in which our Lord
declares the woes of the Scribes and Pharisees, and it is
given in substance by St. Luke, though the latter does
not follow the order in which the woes are given in the
first Gospel, and his account is very much abbreviated.
We would therefore assign this passage also to the Markan
section of the first Gospel ; and if the question be raised why
it does not appear in the second Gospel, we would answer
that the subject-matter of the section, while of extreme
importance to Jews, would be omitted from an edition
prepared for a Gentile Church in Rome, as being of much
less importance and interest to them.   Now if this analysis
of these sections be correct, we are left with a sharp
division between the five blocks of homogeneous ' sayings,'
and the great mass of Markan material into which the
sayings seem to have been thrust.

It is true that much of what we have assigned to the
Markan document is held by critics to have been derived
from Q, and these sections will be duly weighed, but
assuming for the present that the division we have made
is a true division, we now proceed to consider the five
blocks of sayings which we have taken out of the first
Gospel.[1] The very arrangement of a group of five is
significant.   Sir John Hawkins compares with it the five
books of the Pentateuch, the five books of the Psalms,
the five Megilloth, as well as other similar groups, and
concludes by saying : ' It is hard to believe that it is by
accident that we find in a writer with the Jewish affinities
of Matthew this five times repeated formula,' *i.e.* ' When
Jesus had finished these sayings.' Another most significant fact is that, according to Eusebius (iii. 39), Papias
wrote a commentary on the Logia of Matthew in *five*
books, and we may conclude that he did so because the
sayings were already grouped into that number of chapters.

[1] For a detailed analysis of these sections, see Additional Note, p. 93 ff.

All this makes a strong *prima facie* argument that the
Logia of Matthew are not lost, but exist in the first Gospel,
sandwiched between corresponding portions of Markan
narrative. The traditional title of the first Gospel is thus
easily accounted for. If the distinctive portion of the
Gospel had been taken from some Gospel (Q) of unknown
authorship, there is no apparent reason why the name of
St. Matthew should have been attached to it, and if a
work of such first-rate importance as one written by the
apostle Matthew, and containing the discourses of Christ,
was ever in existence, it is hard to believe that it could
have disappeared from among the treasured documents
of the Christian Church. The statement of Papias cannot lightly be set aside, and our analysis of the Gospel
enables us to see that St. Matthew's work has never been
lost, but is still before us in the Gospel which bears his
name.

The history of the Gospel may then be reconstructed
somewhat as follows :—In quite early days St. Matthew
collated the sayings ascribed to Jesus, rejecting those that
were spurious and retaining those that he recognised as
having been spoken at different times by his great Master.
He arranged these according to an approved Jewish method
by placing them in five groups, the sayings in each group
dealing directly with some topic upon which our Lord was
wont to discourse from time to time. When the Church
began to find converts among the Hellenistic Jews of the
Dispersion, translations of these sayings were made, and
one such copy found its way to Egypt, where there were
from earliest times a considerable number of Jews. St.
Mark had already left there a copy of his memoirs of St.
Peter's preaching ; it was not identical with either that
earlier edition which he had left at Caesarea (see chap. v.)
nor with one which he was to publish considerably later in
Rome. It contained parables and other teaching of our
Lord's, which St. Matthew had not included in his work,

and there were in it certain references which would be of
special interest to Christians living in Egypt. It fell to
the lot of some member of this Church to throw into one
volume these two accounts of what Jesus said and what
Jesus did. He accomplished this in a very simple, a very
rough and ready manner, by separating the five chapters
and inserting each at some likely point in the Markan
narrative, but he was always careful to mark the point
of transition by a formula which is found nowhere else.
He also possessed an account of the birth of our Lord
which had been derived through stages of which we have
no trace, from Joseph the husband of the mother of our
Lord, and which, from its inclusion of the flight into Egypt
and other details, seems to have been drawn up in Egypt.[1]
This he naturally prefixed to the other two sections. He
further interpolated quotations from a collection of
Messianic proof-texts at points at which such seemed
appropriate, and to the Gospel thus prepared the name of
' The Gospel according to St. Matthew ' was given to distinguish it from the Gospel according to St. Mark, which by
that time was beginning to be known.

If this account of the way in which St. Matthew's name
was attached to this Gospel be correct, it follows that we
need not seek for any exact definition in time for the
occasions on which the several discourses or the individual
sayings were uttered by our Lord. The relation of saying
to saying is that of its bearing upon the topic which St.
Matthew discovered underlying the general teaching of
Jesus. He would put together sayings some of which were
uttered early in the course of our Lord's ministry, and
others which He uttered on His way to Jerusalem, or in
the course of His latest ministry in the temple.

---

[1] It is interesting to note that while Justin (*Dial.* 77, 78) and Tertullian
(*Jud.* 9) say that the Magi came from Arabia, which lies to the south of
Palestine, the first Gospel says that they came 'from the East.' The two
statements are seen to be in agreement if we accept the theory that the
birthplace of the first Gospel was Alexandria.

Thus we shall still continue to use the term ' The Sermon on the Mount,' but the unity of that sermon is to be ascribed to St. Matthew rather than to the great Teacher whose words he recorded. We need not on this account take up the position that our Lord never delivered a set discourse in which many of these sayings found utterance, but it does not seem likely that we have such a discourse in this ' sermon.' For in the first place no report of that discourse could have been taken down, and it is impossible to accept that any one could have committed it to memory on the strength of a single utterance. In the second place, no amount of editorial freedom would have led St. Luke to separate that discourse into disjointed fragments as, on this hypothesis, he has done. Further, it is extremely difficult to account for the connection of such passages as Matthew v. 31, 32, vi. 7-15, and vii. 7-11 if they formed parts of a single discourse. Those who hold that the sermon was actually delivered as a sermon by our Lord are forced to regard these and other passages as interpolations, but this method of accounting for the collection as it stands raises other difficulties. Then if the arrangement of sayings was the work of our Lord, there is no reason why we should not suppose that the other sections in which we have blocks of sayings in the first Gospel are also given as delivered by Him, and this would produce an impression of Christ's method far different from what we believe was the fact. It would make Him out to be a formalist, whereas the remarks have a spontaneity and freshness about them which make it far more probable that they were uttered as each several occasion demanded, with a readiness suggestive of a fountain of truth which was brimfull, and ever ready to pour forth the riches of its contents.

What then was the ' unity ' which appealed to the mind of St. Matthew, and led him to group together the sayings which make up our ' Sermon on the Mount ' ? The answer varies with the scholar who considers it. Professor

Votaw considers that the theme is sufficiently described under the title ' The Ideal Life,' and the Beatitudes are considered to give a summary of the theme which is afterwards developed in detail. Dr. Stanton describes the theme as ' The Character of the Heirs of the Kingdom,' but this seems more appropriate as a description of chapter xviii. Holtzmann, Wendt, and others find the unity in v. 17-20, and describe it as ' The Fulfilment of the Law.' None of these however seems, to the present writer at least, to supply a sufficient unity. The present Bishop of Oxford comes much nearer to it when he describes it as ' The Moral Law of the Kingdom.' Dr. Gore, however, goes on to say that it is ' law, not grace ; letter, not spirit.' But although we shall acknowledge that it contains what we should expect in a first chapter of discourses on the Kingdom—a statement of its statutes, of the great principles that underlie the whole conception of that great Jewish ideal as it existed in the thought of Christ—it is the *spirit* of the law, rather than its letter that is before us.

The most satisfactory account, which we have seen, of the theme not only of this first chapter of St. Matthew's work, but also of the remaining four sections, is given by Monsignor Barnes in the *Journal of Theological Studies*, 1905. M. Barnes holds that St. Matthew's purpose was to illustrate from the teaching of Jesus His exposition of that idea which was always prominently before the religious conception of the Jew, and which formed the purpose of the preaching of both the Baptist and the Christ—the Kingdom of God. M. Barnes thus arranges the sections :

Matt. v., vi., vii. : The Law of the Kingdom.

Matt. x. : The Rulers of the Kingdom.

Matt. xiii. : The Parables of the Kingdom.

Matt. xviii. : Relations of the Members of the Kingdom.

Matt. xxiv., xxv. : The Coming of the King.

This seems a fair description of the contents of these sections, though others may prefer other titles.

In discussing the Markan narrative which we have in the first Gospel, it will be best to begin with a statement of the points which have secured recognition and acceptance among scholars. These can scarcely be better stated than they are by Dr. Stanton in the work to which frequent reference has been made, and which will long remain a storehouse of scholarly research and critical acumen. Dr. Stanton says :

1. While the narratives of the birth and infancy of Jesus in St. Matthew and St. Luke are widely different, these Gospels begin to agree with one another and with St. Mark from the point at which the latter begins, namely, with the ministry of John the Baptist.

2. By far the greater part of the subject-matter of St. Mark is found in both St. Matthew and St. Luke, and there is on the whole a close parallelism between all three in the arrangement of this matter. In other words, there is a common outline ; into this in St. Matthew and St. Luke a considerable amount of additional matter has been quite diversely introduced.

3. With very few exceptions, our first and third evangelists, so far as they omit incidents and sayings given in St. Mark, do not omit the same ones ; the result being that almost all the sections in St. Mark are found also in one or other of the two remaining Synoptics ; that is to say, there are very few passages peculiar to this Gospel.

4. When the sequence of narratives in St. Matthew or St. Luke differs from that in St. Mark, the other one agrees with St. Mark. In other words, St. Matthew and St. Luke do not, save in one or two

instances, unite against St. Mark as to order. When all three do not agree in respect to it, we have the same sequence in St. Matthew and St. Mark, or in St. Luke and St. Mark.

5. There is further an agreement which is generally considerable, and sometimes very full, between St. Mark and each of the two other Synoptics in the manner in which incidents are related, and in phraseology. All three frequently agree in these respects. But there are also commonly particulars of this kind in which St. Matthew and St. Luke each separately agrees with St. Mark. On the whole the correspondence is closest between St. Matthew and St. Mark ; but there are cases in which the correspondence is closer between St. Luke and the parallel passage in St. Mark than between the latter and the parallel in St. Matthew. Finally, it is to be observed that the amount of agreement in statements or words between St. Matthew and St. Luke alone, in all parts of their Gospels which are in substance contained in St. Mark, is trifling in comparison with the agreement of each separately, and even of both together, with St. Mark.

Dr. Stanton concludes that if we suppose that St. Matthew and St. Luke used Mark, or *a document resembling Mark*, and each in his own way revised and supplemented it, we have a simple and natural explanation of these phenomena. The present writer finds himself in complete agreement with all the facts as related by Dr. Stanton, but in the conclusion drawn he would prefer the second of the alternatives offered by him, and would rather say that the two authors used ' a document resembling St. Mark,' and not the second Gospel as we know it. The reasons for this preference are set forth in the chapter dealing with the

second Gospel, and we proceed now to discuss, in the light
of this preference, the Markan narrative as it appears in the
first.

The first section which we assign to the authorship of
St. Mark is the one which is most disputed, and it raises
most of the questions which gather around the question
of the Markan element in St. Matthew and St. Luke. It
is the section in which the ministry of the Baptist is set
forth with the sequel so closely connected with it—the
temptation of our Lord. The majority of critics refer this
section to Q, and we have already alluded to this in general
terms. A comparison of the three accounts reveals at
once the ground upon which they arrive at their conclusion. By far the fullest account is given by St. Luke,
and this evangelist prefaces his account with a detailed
chronological statement which is a distinct addition of
his own.

The account given in the first Gospel is not quite so
extensive as that in the third Gospel, but it is in close
agreement with it in giving the words of the Baptist in
some detail, and in calling attention to the rebuke given by
the Baptist to the Pharisees and the Sadducees. The
second Gospel gives the account of the Baptist's ministry
in a most scanty fashion. The preaching of the Baptist
is referred to in the very brief statement that he preached
the baptism of repentance for the remission of sins. There
is no reference to the denunciation of the religious leaders
among the Jews. The announcement of the coming of
Jesus varies in precisely the same way in the three accounts.
St. Luke's account is the fullest and St. Mark's the briefest.
At the same time it is to be noticed that both in this and
in the preceding section, where we get a reference to the
same matter in the first Gospel and in the second, whether
it be the description of the habits of the Baptist or of
his reference to the coming Messiah, there is marked
resemblance in phraseology, so that we may infer that if

St. Matthew derived the sections from any one source, St. Mark also must have taken them from that source. In describing the ministry of the coming Messiah, the first Gospel (here in agreement with the third) makes the significant addition that He would baptize 'with fire.' In the baptism of our Lord the first Gospel represents the Baptist as accepting a position of inferiority to Him who came to be baptized. We can see how this would be a point to be insisted upon when addressing those who held John to be 'that prophet' if not the Messiah Himself, and the fulfilling of 'righteousness' would again have weight with those to whom the Old Testament teaching on the subject of righteousness would be familiar. The second Gospel also differs characteristically by the insertion of the word σχιζομένους, 'rent asunder,' where the other Gospels say simply that the heavens 'were opened.' This addition is one of the many vivid details which make up the outstanding feature of the second Gospel. They indicate not only the evidence of an eye-witness, but also the experience of the speaker who has learnt how to make his narrative vivid and effective for his hearers. They are distinctly Petrine in origin, and appear appropriately in the later rather than in the earlier edition of the Petrine memoirs.

The temptation of our Lord sprang directly out of the manifestation made in the course of His baptism, and forms one section with the foregoing. It exhibits precisely the same features as we find in the latter ; a full account in the third Gospel, another almost as full in the first with the reference to 'the holy city' which repeats the Jewish tendency, and an account in the second which by comparison is the merest outline, and gives no details of our Lord's temptation. It exhibits, however, the same vivid touch, which we have already found in the second Gospel, in the statement peculiar to that Gospel that our Lord was 'with the wild beasts.'

Now apparently the reason which leads critics to refer
the whole of this section to Q is the difficulty of finding
a place for it in the Markan source, when that source is
taken to be the canonical Mark. If this section belongs to
that source, then we have the editors of the first and third
Gospels making additions to that source for which no
account can be given. To avoid this difficulty, the whole
section is commonly assigned to Q. And yet if we accept
this, we entirely destroy the character of Q, so far as we
can assign it a definite character. For in this section we
must admit that the proportion of narrative is far in excess
of anything in the nature of discourse. It contains far
more of the words of the Baptist than of the teaching of
Christ, and the very few words of Jesus which it records
differ in what we have seen to be an essential point from
Logia properly so called. They do not deal with essential
spiritual principles, but are dependent for interpretation
upon the circumstances which called them forth. If again
the editors of the first and third Gospels derived the
section from Q, the fact that they differ as they do between
themselves creates a further difficulty. St. Luke treats
his Logian source with the greatest respect. What are
called ' Lukan characteristics ' are least apparent in this
part of his Gospel, which means that he felt less inclined
to use his editorial freedom in amending this one of his
sources. This was only natural to one who realised that
in this he was dealing with ' the words of the Lord Jesus.'
But how then are we to explain the fact that he differs
from St. Matthew as he does if they both used the same
source ? In the teaching of the Baptist, in the order of
the temptations, and in minor details, he seems to be
using a source which, while exhibiting a general likeness
to that used in compiling the first Gospel, nevertheless is
far from being identical with that source.

Now all these difficulties find an easy solution when we
refer this section not to Q, but to Mark, meaning by that

an earlier edition of the work of that evangelist. We see at once that the earlier editions, prepared in Palestine, or for Jews, would be in this section much fuller than they would be in the later edition which belongs to Rome, while the latter would exhibit just those vivid details which we have found in it. We also secure what seems to the present writer the great advantage of considering Q to be homogeneous. It is difficult to answer the objection of those who say that if this narrative section can be allowed at the beginning of Q, there is no reason why we should refuse to admit that it also closed with an account of our Lord's Passion. But if Q contained both these sections it must have been to all intents and purposes 'a Gospel,' and its disappearance and loss becomes inexplicable. Returning to the section as it appears in the first Gospel, we notice that it contains more than one allusion to what we may call a Jewish interest. The denunciation of the religious orders among the Jews and the reference to the 'holy city,' these are things which would appear naturally in an account written for those who were Jewish Christians, and in describing the difference between the baptism of John and the baptism of our Lord, the addition of the significant phrase ' He shall baptise *with fire*,' belongs naturally to an edition prepared for those who had witnessed or heard of what took place at Pentecost and in the house of Cornelius, but the phrase would have lost significance for those who belonged to a later age, and lived in Rome. It therefore fails to appear in the second Gospel. We confidently then refer this section to the Markan source rather than to Q.

The next Markan section in the first Gospel begins at iv. 17-25 and continues on in chapters viii. and ix., the sequence being broken, as we have seen, by the insertion of chapters v., vi., and vii. which are taken from another source. In this passage we notice that the call of the first four disciples while agreeing almost word for word

with what we have in St. Mark does not appear in St.
Luke. This evangelist gives in the fifth chapter of his
Gospel what is evidently a later and more decisive call
than what is given here. The fact of the two calls creates
no difficulty. We can see from the fourth Gospel that
the first attachment of the disciples to Christ was
apparently less binding, and that their connection with
Him became a much closer thing later on. In the first
edition of Mark the later call was described, and as such
appears in the third Gospel, but in the later editions the
earlier call was given.

This is followed by the story of the cure of a leper,
chap. viii. 1-4. The section is given in practically the
same terms in all three accounts, but in the second Gospel
we notice at least two ' vivid touches.' In verse 41 of
that Gospel we read that Christ ' had compassion ' upon
the leper, and in verse 43 a remarkable word [1] is used to
describe the strictness with which Christ charged the man
that he was not to publish his cure abroad. That these
two expressions do not appear in the first Gospel is usually
explained on the ground that they were omitted by its
editor probably for the sake of brevity. But the brevity
so gained would be very slight in amount, and one would
scarcely imagine that to secure this slight advantage words
which have so much to do with the personal feeling of our
Lord would be omitted ; and that St. Luke, writing under
quite different conditions and for a different clientele,
should fix upon precisely the same words to save space
seems to us most unlikely. A far more reasonable
explanation is to suppose that their non-appearance in the
first Gospel is due simply to the fact that they were not
included in the edition of Mark which was used by the
editor. Time had revealed to both St. Peter and St. Mark
that the personality of their Lord was the great treasure
which they had to hand down to the Church, and thus

---

[1] ἐμβριμησάμενος.

that which had to do with the personal life of Christ found
expression in the later edition though it was absent from
the earlier.

The story of the cure of the centurion's servant which
follows is one of the most disputed sections of our Gospel.
It is given both by St. Luke and by the editor of the first
Gospel, but it is completely absent from the second.
On the principle that non-Markan material means Q,
this section also is assigned to the Logian document, and
with Dr. Willoughby Allen we are compelled to ask what
a compilation of discourses can have in common with a
narrative section like this. Dr. Allen points out that
' the central point of the story is not Christ's *saying* " not
even in Israel have I found such faith," for as a saying
apart from its context that has no meaning, but the *facts*
that Christ could heal with a word, and that He had done
such a healing for the servant of a centurion.' To us this
comment of Dr. Allen seems unanswerable, and on the
theory of a deutero-Mark in which the section appeared,
though it was omitted from the trito-Mark, we have no
hesitation in referring this section also to the Markan
document.

From this point to the end of the ninth chapter we have
what is accepted as Markan material. The three versions
differ, as we should expect them to differ, if, while written
down by one man, they were written on different occasions
and for different classes of persons. There are also editorial
changes, especially in the third Gospel, but these need not
detain us.

We have shown that chapters x.-xi. 1 belong to the Logia,
and we have also given reasons for relating the section
which follows this xi. 2-30 to the Markan document. From
xii. 1-xiii. 23 we have a distinct Markan section, only broken
by the insertion of a quotation from the Messianic proof-
texts to which reference has previously been made. In
verses 5-7 of the twelfth chapter we have a statement

made by our Lord which appears in the first Gospel, but
not in the others. The statement carries that Jewish
reference which we have seen is characteristic of the
first Gospel throughout. It reflects upon the attitude of
the religious teachers of the Jews, and would have its
place in a narrative prepared by St. Mark for the Jewish
Christians of Alexandria. It is wholly unnecessary to
refer it to Q. In the parallel section of canonical Mark we
find a statement which is entirely apposite to the discussion
on the Sabbath given by all three evangelists, and yet
the remarkable words do not appear in either the first or
the third Gospel. In Mark ii. 27 we read that ' the
Sabbath was made for man, and not man for the Sabbath.'
Now if canonical Mark was before both the first and the
third Evangelists, it is exceedingly difficult to see on what
ground they omitted the striking words which go so far to
support their own point of view. The so-called ' omissions '
of these evangelists make an insuperable difficulty in the
way of those who accept the theory that canonical Mark
was one of their sources.

In xii. 22-32 we have the account of a discussion which
followed upon the cure of a blind and dumb demoniac.
This section also appears in the second Gospel. Those
who consider that non-Markan material indicates Q assign
this section to that document, and get over the incon-
sistency which might be charged against them by assuming
that in this case St. Mark must have used Q. With reference to the supposed use of Q by St. Mark we have written
elsewhere (see page 109). It is to be noticed that if St.
Mark were here reproducing Q, it is strange that he should
have omitted such striking words as are given in the first
Gospel in verses 27, 28 and 30. Dr. Streeter [1] holds that
St. Mark quoted Q from memory, thus accounting for
passages in which there is a divergence from Q in the
second Gospel, and in any case he contends that St. Mark

[1] *Oxford Studies*, p. 219.

only used the Logian document to a limited extent. But this limited use of sayings in the second Gospel is better accounted for if the point may be conceded that the narrative of an event does not necessarily exclude the words of Jesus uttered on the occasion. This opinion is expressed clearly by Dr. Stanton [1] who says : ' The mere fact of the existence of parallels in the Logian document to sayings contained in St. Mark is no proof that the author of the latter must have derived them from the oral or written Logian collection, and not directly or independently from the Apostle Peter.' This section therefore with the rest we assign to St. Mark's narrative rather than to Q. There are differences between the one account and the other, but these are fully accounted for on the theory of three editions of Mark. The section in which a description of Scribes and Pharisees demanding a sign from our Lord is given does not appear in St. Mark's Gospel, but that need create no difficulty ; for as it has to do with the attitude of these Jews to Christ it would be more apposite in the proto- and deutero-Mark than in the trito-Mark.

The next Markan section of the first Gospel according to our division is found in chapters xii. 33-50 and xiii. 1-23. In this the verses 33-45 in the twelfth chapter do not appear in the second Gospel ; they have the appearance of such sayings as we have found in the five great sections which we have taken to constitute St. Matthew's contribution to this Gospel. But it is clear that they are closely connected with the passage which follows in verses 46-50 which is distinctly Markan, and as they have to do with the spiritual failure of the Scribes and Pharisees, and with our Lord's reflections upon them, it is probable that they were excluded from the trito-Mark for this reason.

xiii. 24-52 is, as we have seen, another of the divisions of this Gospel which close with the formula of transition

[1] *Op. cit.* p. 174.

from sayings to narrative. The fact that one of the
parables—that of the mustard seed—occurs in St. Mark
should not lead us either to include the Matthaean section
in the Markan narrative, or to infer that here St. Mark
is using Q, for there is no reason in the world why we
should rule out from the preaching of St. Peter, reproduced by St. Mark, any parable of our Lord which the
preacher or the evangelist might have thought fit to give.
The parable might have come into the Matthaean Logia
along quite another line of tradition, and there are
linguistic differences between the two accounts which
lead us to infer that this was so. Further, St. Mark
closely connects it with the parable of the seed growing
secretly, and we have shown that if St. Mark derived this
latter parable from Q it is difficult to see why both St.
Matthew and St. Luke should have omitted it in using that
document.

At verse 53 a long section common to the first and
second Gospel begins and continues to xxiv. 36. In the
twentieth, the twenty-second and the twenty-third
chapters occur short sections containing the teaching of
our Lord, which some would on that account refer to Q,
but we have shown reason for including these also in the
Markan document (see p. 68 ff.). A considerable part of
the matter contained in this section does not appear at all
in the third Gospel. It forms what has been called 'the
great omission' from the third Gospel, and a discussion
of it will be found in chapter vi.

It will not be necessary to dwell here upon the differences
between the deutero- and trito-Mark in this section.
They exhibit exactly what, we have seen, might be
expected in the way of difference between one edition and
another—a certain amount of resemblance, inasmuch as
both were the work of one evangelist, but also a certain
amount of difference inasmuch as they were prepared
under different conditions and in the interests of con-

gregations one of which was mainly Jewish, and the other
mainly Gentile. We may notice as confirmatory of this
that the trito-Mark omits the woes spoken by our Lord
against the Scribes and Pharisees.

The last section of the Matthaean Logia begins at xxiv.
37 and continues to xxv. 46. It is what constitutes the
Eschatological section of the first Gospel, although
Eschatological references in the teaching of our Lord are
not limited to this section. The difficult question of the
relation of this discourse to the ' Little Apocalypse ' in the
second Gospel will be better discussed in the following
chapter of this work.

In the concluding section, chapters xxvi. 1 to xxviii. 20,
the correspondence between the first and second Gospels
is particularly close. As we shall see, St. Luke here departs
considerably from the Markan source in relating the
Passion and the post-Resurrection appearances of our
Lord. But the close correspondence between the other
two is of peculiar value to us in view of the fact that the
last chapter of St. Mark has been obviously mutilated.
There can be very little doubt that if we are to seek the
close of the second Gospel we shall find it, with such
variations as we have found between the one edition and
the other, in the first Gospel, and we thus have the
Galilean setting of the Markan narrative unbroken to the
end, while in the third Gospel St. Luke adopts an account
which is far more Judaean than Galilean. The significance
of this will appear in chapter vi.

We may thus conclude that the passages of the first
Gospel which we have been considering are Markan in
origin, but it is obvious that they have not been taken
directly from the second Gospel. In the Additional
Notes appended to the fifth chapter of this work it will be
seen that the points of difference between these sections
and the corresponding passages in Mark are many and
considerable. They are usually accounted for as editorial

alterations of Mark, but such explanations are in the
majority of cases far from satisfactory. They raise as
many difficulties as they remove. If, however, the Markan
narrative in the first Gospel is prior to that which we find
in the second in this sense—that it formed an earlier
edition of St. Mark's work, written when that evangelist
was in Egypt, we have a simple but a satisfactory explanation of both resemblances and divergences, and the
latter will be seen to be just those which would appear
when a writer gives two accounts of the same events, one
account being written on behalf of a Jewish-Christian
community, and the other written at a later date in the
interests of a Gentile Christian Church such as that which
was in existence in Rome about the seventh decade of the
first century.

In making this analysis of the first Gospel we are
perfectly aware that many questions of detail and of
linguistic correspondence and difference have not been
considered. Different scholars have analysed this Gospel
with quite other results. Some of these will be given in
the Additional Notes which follow this chapter. What
has been offered here has been an analysis on broad and
simple lines, taking into account traditional views of the
book and attempting to discover from internal evidence
such a differentiation of the several parts of the Gospel
as will fall in with a reasonable interpretation of that
tradition. It would seem more likely that the books
which make up the Synoptic Gospels were constructed
upon such broad and simple lines, than that they are a
mosaic of small portions of narrative and of discourses
thrown together according to some elaborate plan. Such
a method does not seem to be a likely one in the age in
which these Gospels assumed the form in which we know
them now, and the somewhat mechanical method of
compilation suggested here may after all come nearer the
truth than the more elaborate methods which are offered

by modern scholarship. The present writer is far from disparaging the research of scholars to whom he himself is under such great obligation, but the perils of statistics are well known, and it is possible to build up by the use of verbal categories and the enumeration of vocabularies a structure which will command our respect for the ingenuity of its composer, but which may after all be very far from a true representation of the way in which the Gospels came into being.

ADDITIONAL NOTE I

HARNACK'S RE-ARRANGEMENT OF THE LOGIAN DOCUMENT IN THE FIRST GOSPEL (THE SAYINGS OF JESUS, pp. 127-146.)

1. Matt. iii. 5, 7-12.
2. Matt. iv. 1-11.
3. Matt. v. 1-4, 6, 11, 12.
4. Matt. v. 39-40.
5. Matt. v. 42.
6. Matt. v. 44-48.
7. Matt. vii. 12.
8. Matt. vii. 1-5.
9. Matt. xv. 14.
10. Matt. x. 24-25.
11. Matt. vii. 16-18, xii. 33.
12. Matt. vii. 21, 24-27.
13. Matt. vii. 28, viii. 5-10, 13.
14. Matt. xi. 2-11.
15. Matt. xi. 16-19.
16. Matt. x. 7.
17. Matt. viii. 19-22.
18. Matt. ix. 37-38.
19. Matt. x. 16^a.
20. Matt. x. 12, 13.

21. Matt. x. 10^b.
22. Matt. x. 15.
23. Matt. xi. 21-23.
24. Matt. x. 40.
25. Matt. xi. 25-27.
26. Matt. xiii. 16, 17.
27. Matt. vi. 9-13.
28. Matt. vii. 7-11.
29. Matt. xii. 22, 23, 25, 27, 28, 30, 43-45.
30. Matt. xii. 38, 39, 41, 42.
31. Matt. v. 15.
32. Matt. vi. 22, 23.
33. Matt. xxiii. 4, 13, 23, 25, 27, 29, 30, 32, 34-36.
34. Matt. x. 26-33.   (b) Matt. xii. 32.
35. Matt. vi. 25-33.
36. Matt. vi. 19-21.
37. Matt. xxiv. 43-51.
38. Matt. x. 34-36.

39. Matt. v. 25-26.
40. Matt. xiii. 31-33.
41. Matt. vii. 13, 14.
42. Matt. viii. 11, 12.
43. Matt. xxiii. 37-39.
44. Matt. xxiii. 12.
45. Matt. x. 37.
46. Matt. x. 38.
47. Matt. v. 13.
48. Matt. xviii. 12, 13.
49. Matt. vi. 24.

50. Matt. xi. 12, 13.
51. Matt. v. 18.
52. Matt. v. 32.
53. Matt. xviii. 17.
54. Matt. xviii. 15, 21, 22.
55. Matt. xvii. 20[b].
56. Matt. xxiv. 26-28, 37-41.
57. Matt. x. 39.
58. Matt. xxv. 29.
59. Matt. xix. 28.

For a criticism of the above see Dr. Willoughby C. Allen in *Oxford Studies*, pp. 235-272. Dr. Allen offers an alternative rearrangement which may be examined by the student and compared with Harnack's as given above.

Dr. Burkitt considers that if we wish to reconstruct the order and arrangement of the lost document used by Matthew and Luke (he will not call it the Logia), we must take the outline of it from Luke rather than from Matthew. We must subtract from Luke the first two chapters, and those sections of the third Gospel which are derived from Mark: what is left will give us an approximate outline of the document in question. In this Dr. Burkitt is in agreement with Dr. Armitage Robinson. See *The Gospel History in Transmission*, pp. 130 ff.

Dr. Stanton also seems to prefer St. Luke in analysing the Logian source known to the first and third evangelists. His analysis of this source in the first Gospel is as follows :—

1. The ushering in of the Ministry of Christ: Matt. iii. 5, 7-12, 13-17 and iv. 1-11[a].

2. The first stage in the Preaching of the Gospel: Matt. v. 3 ; vi. 8 ; vi. 16-18 ; vii. 1-5, 12, 15-21, 24-27 ; viii. 5-10, 13 ; xi. 2-11, 16-19.

3. The Extension of the Gospel: Matt. ix. 35 ; viii. 19-22 ; ix. 37, 38 ; x. 5[a], 7-16, 40.

4. The Rejection and the Reception of Divine truth: Matt. xi. 21-23, 25-27 ; xiii. 16, 17.

5. Instruction on Prayer: Matt. vi. 9-13 ; vii. 7-11.

6. Jesus and His Antagonists: Matt. xxii. 34-40 ; xii. 22-30, 43-45, 39-42 ; vi. 22, 23 ; xxiii. 136.

7. Exhortations to disciples in view of the opposition and

other trials that awaited them : Matt. x. 26-33 ; xii. 32 ; vi. 25-34, 19-21 ; xxiv. 43-44, 45-51 ; x. 34-38 ; xiii. 31-33 ; xviii. 5-7, 15, 21, 22 ; xvii. 19-20.

8. The doom on Jerusalem, and the things of the end : Matt. xxiii. 37-39 ; xxiv. 26-28, 37-41.

Dr. Stanton adds that there may be among pieces peculiar to St. Matthew or St. Luke a few derived from this source which are not included in the above.   But the amount of such matter is not likely to have been considerable.   In the *Oxford Studies of the Synoptic Problem* Dr. Willoughby Allen criticises Harnack's reconstruction of the Book of Sayings, and offers an alternative of his own based on the principle that the sayings in Matthew, over and above those already found in Mark, when put together present us with a homogeneous, consistent and intelligible work (no doubt only fragmentary). This source, he holds, was a collection of Christ's sayings and discourses compiled to represent certain aspects of His teaching, and was marked by a very characteristic phraseology.   Dr. Allen's reconstruction of this source is as follows :

1. Matt. **v.** 3-12.   Nine Beatitudes.
> 17, 20, 21-24, 27-28, 31-32, 33-48.   The old Law and new righteousness.

vi. 1-6, 16-18 ; **vii.** 1-5, 6, 12, 15-16, 21-23.   Illustrations of the better righteousness.

vii. 24-27.   Concluding parable.

ix. 37-38 ; **x.** 5ᵇ-8 ; **x.** 12-13, 15-16, 23.   The Mission of the Disciples.

x. 24-41.   A Discourse about Persecution.

xi. 2-11, 12-15, 16-19.   Discourse about John the Baptist.

xi. 20-30.   Woes upon certain cities followed by thanksgiving to the Father.

xii. 27-28, 30, 32, 33-37.   A Discourse about Beelzebub.

xii. 38-45.   Discourse in answer to request for a sign.

xiii. 24-33, 26-52.   Parables concerning the Kingdom.

xviii. 15-20 ; **xviii.** 21-35.   A Discourse on forgiveness.

xxiii. 2-36.   A Denunciation of the Pharisees.

Matt. xxiv. 10-12, 26-28, 30, 37-41, 43-51; xxv. 1-12, 14-
46.   Eschatological Sayings.

    v. 13-16, 18-19, 25-26, 29-30; vi. 7-8, 9-13, 14-15,
19-34; vii. 7-11, 13-14, 16-19.   Fragments
inserted by editor in the Sermon on the Mount.

viii. 11-12, 19-22; ix. 13; xii. 5-7, 11-12; xiii. 16-17.

xv. 13-14; xvi. 17-19; xviii. 7, 10-12-14; xix. 11-12,
28.

xxiii. 37-39.   Detached Sayings, which stood in the
source in positions which we cannot rediscover.

xx. 1-15; xxi. 28-32; xxii. 2-14.   Other parables.

Dr. Allen is more consistent than most critics in omitting from
the Logia sections which really belong to the Narrative Source,
but it does not appear to the present writer that he has
accounted for the tradition which connects the name of St.
Matthew with the first Gospel, and it seems more likely that
the compilation of that Gospel was a more simple matter
than the somewhat elaborate arrangement here suggested.
Dr. Allen marks certain words and phrases as characteristic
of this source.   They are such as ἡ βασιλεία τῶν οὐρανῶν, ὁ
πατὴρ ὑμῶν ὁ ἐν οὐρανοῖς, δικαιοσύνη, ὁμοιόω, ὁ υἱὸς τοῦ
ἀνθρώπου, ἔμπροσθεν c. Gen., πονηρός, οἱ ὑποκριταί, ἡ παρουσία
τοῦ υἱοῦ τοῦ ἀνθρώπου.   It does not seem, however, that too
much weight should be given to a vocabulary of this sort.
Such words belong to the phraseology commonly used in such
teaching as our Lord would give, and they would inevitably
appear in any collection of sayings, however formless and
inconsecutive they might be.   To us it seems more likely that
the arrangement should be assigned to St. Matthew, the
language to his translator, or the editor of the Gospel as we
know it.   But, if arrangement belongs to the Apostle, then the
arrangement of five blocks should be taken into account.

ADDITIONAL NOTE II

ANALYSIS OF ST. MATTHEW'S FIVE COLLECTIONS
OF SAYINGS OF JESUS

SECTION 1, MATT. v., vi., vii.

v. 1. εἰς τὸ ὄρος. Luke has ἔστη ἐπὶ τόπου πεδινοῦ. The eight
beatitudes in Matt. are represented by only three in
Luke. In Luke the disciples are directly addressed, and
the beatitudes are followed by corresponding woes.

3. τῷ πνεύματι, an interpretation of πτωχοί, which may
have been in the source, or may have been added by
St. Matthew.

4. πενθοῦντες . . . παρακληθήσονται. In Luke we read
κλαίοντες . . . γελάσατε, κλαίειν is frequent in Luke,
and γελᾶν would follow by antithesis, but the expressions
are Hebraistic (cf. Ps. cxxvi. 6, Eccl. iii. 4), and may
have been in the source.

11. ψευδόμενοι does not appear elsewhere in the Synoptists,
and the word reads as if it were an interpolation. It is
omitted in D. Latt. and Syrs. The wording of this verse
in Luke is entirely different. We infer from this not
that St. Luke altered Q, but that he used a different
collection of Logia. See p. 56 ff.

12. ἀγαλλιᾶσθε, Luke σκιρτήσατε. Cf. Luke i. 41, 44 and
Psalm 68, 16.

13-16. Two brief parables. The former is given by St. Luke
in xiv. 34 as having been spoken on the way from Galilee
to Jerusalem. It also appears in Mark ix. 50, but it
does not follow from this that St. Mark took it from Q.
See p. 109. The second is given by St. Luke in viii. 16
with considerable verbal differences. It also appears in
Mark. iv. 21 where it is thrown into the form of a
question, and seems to be quite independent of the statements made in Matt. and Luke.

17-48. Relation of the New Law of the Kingdom to the Old
Law.

18. Appears in St. Luke's account of the journey up to
Jerusalem.

v. 20. Note as a Matthaean characteristic the condemnation of the Scribes and Pharisees.

21-24. These sayings do not appear at all in Luke. Why should he have omitted them if they belonged to a source which was common to him and to St. Matthew?

25-26. Derived by St. Luke from 'the Travel Document,' xii. 58. The wording varies in the two versions. Matt. has ἴσθι εὐνοῶν τῷ ἀντιδίκῳ, while Luke has δὸς ἐργασίαν ἀπηλλάχθαι αὐτοῦ. So also where Matt. has ὑπηρέτης, Luke has πράκτωρ.

27-28. This saying is not given by St. Luke. See note on vv. 21-24.

29-30. This passage appears as a 'Doublet' in chap. xix. 9, which latter is a Markan Section. Cf. Mark x. 11, and Luke xvi. 18. It is to be noticed that Matthew adds the words παρεκτὸς λόγου πορνείας. This is in keeping with his Jewish 'Tendency.' See Allen, I.C.C. in loco.

33-37. Not in Luke.

38-40. Luke vi. 29.

41-42. ῥαπίζειν, elsewhere only in Matt. xxvi. 17.

41. Not in Luke.

43-48. Luke vi. 27-36.

Matt. has ἔσεσθε τέλειοι, but Luke has γίνεσθε οἰκτείρμονες; which last word appears only here in the Gospels. To take this as a deliberate alteration on the part of St. Luke can hardly be justified.

vi. 1-18. Warnings against hypocrisy. Dr. Wright says that this section contains 'foreign matter,' and that Matt. vi. 7-15 is 'out of place.' But this criticism presupposes a stricter coherence than is to be expected from the character of the source used by St. Matthew. See p. 56 ff.

1-8. Does not occur in Luke. It is difficult to think that he would have omitted them, if he had used either the first Gospel or the same collection of Sayings as St. Matthew used.

9-15. We find in Luke that this model Prayer was given on an occasion when the disciples asked their Master to teach them to pray. Luke xi. 2-4. The version he gives contains only three petitions and no doxology. The latter seems to be an addition even in the Matthaean text. See *Comm. in loco*. In the Lukan version of the first petition there is a remarkable variant found in Gregory of Nyssa, which reads as follows :—ἐλθέτω τὸ ἅγιον πνεῦμα ἐφ᾽ ἡμᾶς καὶ καθαρισάτω ἡμᾶς.

vi. 11. ἐπιούσιον. See *Comm. and Wright in loco*. It is impossible that St. Luke made all these alterations and omissions if the details given us in Matt. had appeared in his source also. We conclude that he used a different source.

16-18. Not in Luke.

19-33. The importance of the spiritual.

19-21. Luke xii. 32. Note difference of wording.

22-23. Luke xi. 34, 35.

24. Luke xvi. 13.

25-33. Of this passage too Dr. Wright says that it is 'out of place.' See note on vi. 1-18. It appears in Luke in xii. 22.

vii. 1-12. The Laws of the Kingdom.

1-5. The Law concerning Censoriousness. Luke vi. 37-38. The section which follows in Luke is given in Matt. in xv. 14 and x. 24 ff. A clear indication of the non-chronological character of the source, and of the difference between this and the source used by St. Luke.

6. The Law of Sacrilege. Not in Luke.

7-11. The Law concerning Prayer. Luke xi. 9-13.

12. The Golden Rule. Luke vi. 31.

13-23. Warnings.

13-14. This appears in Luke xiii. 22-25.

15. Not in Luke.

16-19. Luke vi. 43-45. The passage in Matt. xii. 33-35 contains similar teaching, but it is not a true doublet. The figure was one which might have been used by our Lord with incidental variations.

22-23. St. Luke takes this from 'the Travel Document.' xiii. 26.

24-27. Concluding similitude. Given in Luke with differences in wording which we account for on the ground not of alterations made by St. Luke, but of a difference in the sources. See p. 56 ff.

28-viii. 1. An editorial note marking a transition from

discourse to narrative. The phrase καὶ ἐγένετο ὅτε
ἐτέλεσεν is Hebraistic. See Dalman, *Words of Jesus*,
p. 32.

SECTION 2, ix. 37–x. 42.

ix. 37-38. St. Luke gives this (x. 1) as a remark made to the
Seventy, but Matthew gives it as addressed to the
Twelve, and follows it with an account of the call of the
Twelve and of Christ's charge to them.

x. 1. Luke ix. 1.

7-10. Luke ix. 2-3, but part of verse 10 appears in Luke as
addressed to the Seventy.

7. St. Luke gives this charge in brief and general terms,
but adds the characteristic word ἰᾶσθαι.

11. Appears in Luke ix. 4-6 as spoken to the Twelve.

12-15. Appears in Luke as spoken to the Seventy (x. 5-12).

16. Appears in Luke as spoken to the Seventy (x. 3).

17-22. This does not appear in Luke at all. Dr. Wright
describes it as a Markan addition. It is true that Mark
has a similar passage (xiii. 9 ff.), but the introduction of
the Logion here indicates another source. That a
similar saying should appear in Markan narrative does
not imply that St. Mark used Q. St. Peter might well
quote such a saying of our Lord's in the course of his
preaching.

23. This is an eschatological saying which St. Matthew
inserts here as an appropriate conclusion to the passage.

24. This is inserted by St. Luke in the sermon on the
Plain (vi. 40).

25. ἀρεκτὸν τῷ μαθητῇ ἵνα γένηται ὡς ὁ διδάσκαλος appears
in Luke as κατηρτισμένος πᾶς ἔσται ὡς ὁ διδάσκαλος. The
word κατηρτισμένος appears only here in the Gospels,
though it is not uncommon in the Pauline letters. The
word ἀρεκτόν is found only in Matt.

26-33. St. Luke gives this as a part of the address to the
Twelve (xii. 3 ff.) The Lukan form differs from the
Matthaean. St. Luke has five sparrows for two farthings.
Harnack describes this variant as 'an enigma,' and asks
whether sparrows had become cheaper when St. Luke
wrote! To such straits are critics reduced when they

insist upon the theory that the editors of the first and
third gospels used the same Logian source, or Q, and
that variants imply emendation.

x. 34-36. Luke xii. 49-53. Where Matthew has μάχαιραν,
Luke has διαμερισμόν.

37-39. This appears in Luke as spoken when Christ was
journeying up to Jerusalem (xiv. 25-27). As verse 38
appears also in Mark (viii. 35), we are not surprised to
find that it occurs as a doublet in both Matthew and
Luke. The occurrence of the Pauline words περιποιεῖσθαι
and ζωογονεῖν in the Lukan version is to be noted. See
Acts xx. 28 and 1 Tim. iii. 13 for the one, and Acts. vii.
19 and 1 Tim. 6, 13 for the other. They do not occur
elsewhere in the Gospels.

40. The passage in xviii. 5 is not a true doublet. The
sayings seem rather to have been uttered by our Lord on
different occasions, and St. Mark followed by St. Luke
has run the two sayings together.

41. Does not occur at all in St. Luke.

42. This also does not appear in St. Luke's Gospel. It
occurs in St. Mark's (ix. 41), but it does not follow
either that St. Matthew derived it from St. Mark, or
that the latter obtained it from Q.

xi. 1. Note the formula of transition from discourse to narrative ; and compare xiii. 53 and xix. 1.

The way in which throughout this section some of these
sayings are given by St. Luke as spoken to the Twelve,
others as spoken to the Seventy, while others again are
given as spoken on quite other occasions, while St.
Matthew gives them all as spoken to the Twelve Disciples,
is strongly confirmatory of the contention that each took
the sayings from different collections of Logia, in which
the occasion of utterance was not marked. St. Matthew,
as making a topical arrangement of sayings, brings them
all under one head.

SECTION 3, xiii. 16-53.

St. Matthew has attached to the Markan section which
contains the parable of the Sower and its interpretation the

following additional parables which he took from his Logian source.

v. 16-17. Luke gives this as spoken on the way up to Jerusalem when the Seventy returned from their mission.

18-23. The interpretation of the parable of the Sower. The difference in phraseology between this account and that which appears in Mark, especially in the introductory words, seems to indicate that the two accounts are from different sources. That there should be a considerable amount of agreement is not to be wondered at. It does not necessarily indicate a common origin.

24-30. Parable of the Tares. In St. Mark's gospel the parable of the Sower is followed by that of the Seed growing secretly, and this latter is peculiar to Mark. This is a clear indication that there is no common origin for the two sections. It is difficult to see why St. Matthew should have omitted the latter if it was in his source. The parable of the Tares is not, as some would assume, a variant of the parable of the Seed growing secretly. Each parable illustrates the tendency of the two evangelists. St. Matthew inserts the one because it illustrates the corruption of Judaism. St. Mark inserts the other because it accounts for the spontaneous answer of the human heart,—Gentile though it may be—to the appeal of the Gospel—the good seed of the Kingdom.

31-32. The parable of the Mustard Seed. (Mark. iv. 30-32. Luke xiii. 18-19.) All three accounts vary, and St. Luke places the parable in his account of the journey up to Jerusalem. This parable then is from three different sources. St. Mark's source is Petrine. St. Matthew derives it from the Logia; St. Luke gets it from 'the Travel Document.'

33. The parable of the Leaven. Luke xiii. 20-21.

34-35. An insertion from the collection of Messianic Texts.

36-43. Interpretation of the parable of the Tares.

44. Parable of the hidden Treasure. Peculiar to Matthew.

45-46. Parable of the Pearl of great Price. Peculiar to Matthew.

47-50. Parable of the Drawnet. Peculiar to Matthew.

51-52. The Householder and his Treasury.

53. Formula of transition from discourse to Narrative. Note
the word μετῆρεν found in only these formulae, cf. vii. 28.

SECTION 4, xviii. 1–xix. 1.

v. 1-11. A discourse on true greatness. Considerable portions
of this are common to all three evangelists; but Matthew
differs so much from the other two, both in what appears
and what does not, while in addition he gives quite
another occasion for the giving of the discourse, that it
is best to consider the rest of this chapter to belong to
the Matthaean Logia. That it should also appear in the
Markan narrative (with variants) should create no
difficulty. Why should not St. Peter have given the
gist of this teaching in the course of his preaching?
The latter part of the section dealing with 'offences'
was given very briefly in the proto-Mark. See Luke
xvii. 2.

12-14. Parable of the Lost Sheep. Taken by St. Matthew
from the Logia. St. Luke has substantially the same
parable; but he derives it from 'the Travel Document,'
and it appears in xv. 3-7.

15-22. The Law of Forbearance. There is a brief statement
to the same effect in Luke xvii. 3-4. St. Matthew
follows the enunciation of the law with the parable of the
Unforgiving Servant, which does not appear elsewhere.
Note the phrase συναίρειν λόγον which occurs again in
Matthew xxv. 19, another of the five sections of
St. Matthew's collections, and not elsewhere.

23-35. The parable of the Unforgiving Servant.

xix. 1. Formula of transition to Markan narrative. Note the
repetition of μετῆρεν. See note on vii. 28.

SECTION 5, xxiv. 37–xxvi. 1.

The close correspondence between what precedes this section
with the Markan parallel, which is given by St. Luke also,
forbids our assigning it to the Logia of St. Matthew. But at
verse 37 the editor of the first gospel departs from his Markan

source, and what follows may be assigned to the Logia. The
editor seems to have joined on to Christ's words as to the
destruction of Jerusalem His teaching with reference to the
Parousia. Probably the Apocalyptic language used of both events
suggested his doing this.

v. 37. In Luke the phrase ἡ παρουσία τοῦ υἱοῦ τοῦ ἀνθρώπου
appears as ἐν ταῖς ἡμέραις τοῦ υἱοῦ τοῦ ἀνθρώπου. There is
no reason whatever why St. Luke should have altered the
word παρουσία, if he found it in his source. Harnack
says that he abandoned it because it belonged to the
sphere of Jewish Messianic dogma, and was an unsuitable
term for that second coming in which Christians believed.
It is difficult to see how Harnack can hold this opinion
in view of St. Paul's use of the word. See 1 Thess. ii. 20
and elsewhere.

33. At this point St. Luke inserts an additional parallel from
the history of Lot. If the two evangelists used a
common source in which it appeared, it is hard to say
why St. Matthew should have omitted to give it. If it
was not in the source, then it is equally hard to say
whence St. Luke derived it. To account for it as a
'scrap of oral tradition' begs the whole question of an
oral basis for the Gospels, and against this there is too
much to be said. See Chapter i., Additional Note.

40. Where Matthew has ἐν τῷ ἀγρῷ Luke has ἐπὶ κλίνης.
Harnack thinks that St. Luke altered Q in this way so
as to convey the idea that the coming might be at night.
This seems to be an unnecessary refinement of criticism.

43-51. This Logion appears in Luke in 'the Travel Document,'
xii. 39-40.

xxv. 1-13. The parable of the Ten Virgins. This is peculiar to
Matthew. It is appropriate to him as it records the
failure of the Jews to welcome the Messiah.

14-30. The parable of the Talents. In spite of the general
likeness between this parable and that of the Pounds
(Luke xix. 11-26), we do not hold that the two parables
are identical. The Lukan parable appears to be taken
from 'the Travel Document.' It was spoken at Jericho in
the house of Zacchaeus, and all the details of the two
parables differ. The parable of the Pounds in Luke

seems to be based upon the history of the effort of
Archelaus to obtain the title of βασιλεύς. See Commentaries. If the parables are identical and from the
same source, then St. Luke has allowed himself an
altogether unwonted amount of licence in the alteration
of details. It is better to consider that the two accounts
not only differ in origin, but were spoken on different
occasions. Their common theme is that of privilege and
responsibility, and on that subject we may imagine that
our Lord would frequently speak.

31-46. The Last Judgment. Peculiar to Matthew.

xxvi. 1. Formula of transition. See note on vii. 28.

ADDITIONAL NOTE III

QUOTATIONS FROM THE OLD TESTAMENT IN
THE FIRST GOSPEL

A marked feature of the first Gospel is to be found in the
way in which passages from the Old Testament are woven into
the narrative. A distinction, however, has to be drawn between
citations which are given as made by our Lord Himself in the
course of His ministry, whether of teaching or of healing, and
those passages which are evidently introduced by the unknown
editor of the Gospel as we have it. The connection of the
former with what precedes is always such as would be naturally
used by a speaker who wished to point his remarks from the
authoritative literature of his people, but the latter are invariably introduced by the phrase 'that it might be fulfilled
which was spoken by the prophet,' or its equivalent. The
passages are as follows :—

> Matt. i. 22, 23. = Isaiah vii. 14.
>   ii. 5, 6. = Micah v. 1, 4ᵃ.
>   15. = Hosea xi. 1.
>   17, 18. = Jerem. xxxi. 15.
>   23.
>   iv. 14, 16. = Isaiah viii. 23.
>   viii. 17. = Isaiah liii. 4.

Matt. xii. 17-21. = Isaiah xlii. 1-4.
     xiii. 35.
     xxi. 4, 5. = Isaiah lxii. 11 ; Zech. lx. 9.
   xxvii. 9-10.

Of these it is to be noticed

1. That the passage from ii. 23 does not occur in any book of the Old Testament.

2. That the passages in Matt. ii. 6, 15, viii. 17 are apparently cited from a different text from that which we have, as there is considerable difference between the quotation and the passages with which they are usually identified.

3. That the passage in Matt. xxvii. 9 is said to be taken from the prophet Jeremiah, whereas it seems rather to correspond, and that not very closely, to Zechariah xi. 13.

4. In the passage in xiii. 35 the Sinaitic manuscript reads Ἡσαίου τοῦ προφήτου, and Dr. Hort seems to consider it the true reading. If so then a passage is assigned to Isaiah which is really taken from Psalm lxviii. 2.

5. The quotations are made usually from the Hebrew, but some of the passages seem to be taken from the LXX. This is notably the case in Matt. iii. 3 and i. 23, though some other passages also read as if they were reminiscences of the LXX. On the other hand the passages given as quoted by our Lord are wholly from the LXX. They belong, as it seems, to the Markan source used by the editor of the first Gospel, the fuller citations found in Matt. xiii. 14, 15 and xix. 18, 19 being due not to the editor, but to the source ; that source was not canonical Mark, but an earlier edition prepared especially for Jewish Christians, and for that reason making a fuller reference to the Jewish scriptures. We need not therefore make any further reference to these passages.

Returning to the other class we may draw from the facts enumerated above the conclusion that these quotations were made from a collection of similar passages taken from the Hebrew. Dr. Stanton considers that they came before the editor in a translation from an Aramaic document, which may be described as ' a Catena of fulfilments of prophecy,' and this description would account for the features which they exhibit. Probably the name of the prophets, from whose writings the quotations were made, had not been attached to them in this

Catena, and we can account thus for the uncertainty as to origin which some of them exhibit. Dr. Stanton holds that the collection was not a bare Catena, but that the incident which was held to fulfil the prophecy was in each case attached. It is, however, scarcely possible from such slender material as we possess to reconstruct even in outline the contents of the source. It may have been full, or it may have been a very incomplete collection. The paucity of passages referring to the Passion and Crucifixion of our Lord would indicate that it was very imperfect. Dr. Burkitt considers that possibly the compilation was made by St. Matthew, and that it was because of the use made of it in the first Gospel that the name of that apostle was attached to the Gospel. This, however, seems to us a very slender cause for giving St. Matthew's name to the Gospel, and we have indicated a far more likely reason for his name being connected with it. See pages, 72, 73.

CHAPTER V

THE SECOND GOSPEL

THE priority of St. Mark's Gospel is now generally accepted by modern critics. Out of 661 verses in that Gospel all but 50 are to be found in Matthew and Luke, and this incorporated matter so often reveals a marked similarity, not merely in order of arrangement, but also in vocabulary, that the conclusion is inevitable that the first and third evangelists considered the Markan narrative which they thus used to be authoritative. Their respect for the document shows itself in the inclusion in their Gospels of many words and phrases which we should have expected them to alter in the use of their editorial capacity. Thus in Mark ii. 1-12=Matthew ix. 1-8=Luke v. 17-26 we have an account of the healing of a paralytic man in which the awkward parenthesis, ' then saith He to the sick of the palsy,' is reproduced. In Mark ii. 20=Matthew ix. 15= Luke v. 35 the removal of the bridegroom is spoken of by the use of the rare word $ἀπαρθῇ$. The expression ' to taste of death ' is metaphorical, and its alteration by subsequent editors might have been expected, yet it occurs in all three Gospels (Mark ix. 1=Matt. xvi. 28=Luke ix. 27). The same thing occurs where one or other of the two reproduces Markan matter. In Mark xiv.20=Matthew xxvi. 23 the words $ἐμβάπτω$ and $τρύβλιον$ appear, though they are not found in the rest of the New Testament writings ; and in Mark xiii. 33=Luke xxi. 36 we have the word $ἀγρυπνεῖτε$, which does not appear elsewhere in the Synoptic Gospels. It has also been pointed out

that where all three Gospels quote from the Old Testament
the citations are invariably from the LXX.

Now if the common Markan matter presented invariably
such correspondences the conclusion would have been
easily drawn that the two later editors had used canonical
Mark, and had transferred this Gospel *en bloc* to their
writings. But side by side with these resemblances there
occur equally distinct divergences. Matter contained in
Mark is omitted by both the first and the third evangelists.
Outstanding examples of these are :

1. The parable of the Seed growing secretly (iv. 26-29).
2. The healing of the blind man at Bethsaida (viii. 22-26).
3. The reference to the young man with the linen cloth
   (xiv. 51-52).

Again matter contained in Mark is omitted by one or
other of the two later evangelists. The chief instance of
this is to be found in what is called ' the great Lukan
omission' (Mark vi. 45-viii. 26). The passage contains
much that would make it peculiarly worthy of being
transcribed by St. Luke with his appreciation of the
Gentile mission of St. Paul, and with his marked sympathy with women. In addition to the story of the
Syrophenician woman it contains also much teaching on ceremonial defilement, and this again would be
welcomed by one who was in sympathy with St. Paul's
attitude to the Mosaic Law. Explanations of its
omission by St. Luke are forthcoming, and these will
be examined later on, but it will be sufficient here to
record the fact as an outstanding instance of St. Luke's
divergence from the second Gospel as we know it.

There is yet a third class of passages in which the first
and third evangelists seem to depart from a Markan
source. They do this of course in all passages which
belong to the second document or collection of Logia.
But even in narrative portions we come upon cases in which

Matthew and Luke contain incidents which do not appear
in Mark.   A good example of this kind of passage is found
in the healing of the son (servant) of the centurion.   It is
true that in the third Gospel we have a whole section, and
a very considerable one, in which St. Luke has embodied
the account of our Lord's journey from Galilee through
Perea to Jerusalem, and an additional section appearing
in the third Gospel would present no great difficulty.   But
such additional narratives are not found in Matthew,
and Luke's ' Travel Document ' is from a distinct section
in his Gospel.   The similarity between Matthew's description of the healing of the centurion's servant, and that
which appears in the third Gospel, makes it almost certain
that the two evangelists derived it from a common source,
and the question arises what could this source have been ?
In the first Gospel it appears sandwiched between the
story of the healing of the leper, and the recovery of the
mother of Peter's wife, which are both Markan sections.
And yet the incident does not appear in St. Mark's Gospel
as we know it.   Here again we must reserve the discussion
of this fact for a later section of the present work.   It is
mentioned now by way of illustration of points of divergence
from Markan narrative on the part of the other evangelists.
Such differences have greatly complicated the Synoptic
Problem, and it is not surprising that some scholars have
held that the priority of Mark cannot be granted, while
others have held that such differences can only be explained
on the assumption that all three evangelists drew from
another source earlier than all three.   The former account
for what, on their theory, are *additions* made by St. Mark,
the latter for what appear to be *omissions* discovered in
his Gospel.

The chief exponent of the theory that St. Mark was
dependent upon the first Gospel is Zahn,[1] who finds that in
many points Mark is secondary to Matthew.   We shall

[1] See p. 62.

not follow Zahn in discussing this point. His position is not accepted by the great majority of scholars. Those who wish to consider the matter will find the arguments against his contention admirably set forth by Dr. Stanton.[1] For our purposes it is sufficient to point out that the absence from Mark of so much matter that is contained in Matthew is inexplicable on this theory, and though some scholars take a different view, we shall see that there is no good reason for supposing that St. Mark used Q[2] in the preparation of his Gospel. His neglect of the Sayings in the form in which they appear in Matthew can scarcely be accounted for if Matthew was before him when he wrote. At the same time most scholars point out that there are in the narratives given us by St. Mark certain secondary elements. Thus Dr. P. W. Schmiedel says that it is not possible to assign to Mark priority at all points, and that in the light of secondary passages canonical Mark is a later edition. So also Dr. Salmon holds that canonical Mark is ' at once the oldest and the youngest of the Synoptics.' Now this conflicting feature of the second Gospel may be explained without resort to the difficult theory that Matthew is prior to Mark. It is possible that St. Mark prepared his ' Memoirs of St. Peter's preaching '[3] more than once for the benefit of the different churches with which he was associated ; and, if canonical Mark was the latest of the three editions thus prepared, it will be just as we should expect that secondary elements should appear in it. They would thus be secondary, not to the first Gospel, but to that Markan portion which appears in it.

Others, however, consider that all the resemblances as well as the differences are accounted for on the supposition that no one of the three evangelists was dependent upon any one of the others, but that all three used freely an earlier Gospel which corresponded most closely to the

[1] *Op. cit.* p. 38 ff.   [2] See pp. 109, 110.   [3] τὰ ἀπομνημονεύματα.

second Gospel, and which contained both narrative and discourses. The common origin would account for the resemblances, and editorial freedom in selection would account for the differences. This theory has been called the theory of an ' Ur-Markus ' or original Mark. It has never gained any great amount of acceptance in England, though German scholars have felt its attractiveness. We do not advocate its acceptance, for it is inconceivable that if such a Gospel ever existed it should have disappeared without the slightest reference to it having appeared in the early writings of the Christian Church. Dr. Sanday rejects the theory of an Ur-Markus, because the great majority of the coincidences seem to belong to a later form of text rather than to an earlier. He calls this form of text ' a recension,' because ' there is so much method and system about it that it looks like the deliberate work of an editor, or scribe exercising to some extent editorial functions ' (p. 21). Dr. Schmiedel says that ' the difficulty with which the hypothesis can be made to work is increased if we suppose that this original Mark was nearly equal to the canonical Mark.' It becomes difficult to understand why a new book so little different from the old should have been written. If the original was longer than canonical Mark, it becomes possible to assign to it a considerable number of sections (now preserved only in Matthew and Luke) not so easily explained as derived from Matthew's and Luke's other sources. If it were shorter, then the additions of canonical Mark are merely the verses peculiar to him, and these are so very few, that a new book would hardly have been deemed necessary for their incorporation.

The theory which the present work upholds is one which, we claim, retains the great advantages of the Ur-Markus in accounting for the differences between the three Gospels, and yet avoids the many disadvantages which, as we have seen, belong to the hypothesis. It consists in an application of the Proto- Deutero- and Trito-Mark,

with which Dr. Arthur Wright has made us familiar, not
to oral tradition as he makes it, but to documents. This
theory has also been advanced by M. Barnes in two articles
which appeared in the *Monthly Review* in 1904. Before we
proceed to consider it in detail, there are one or two
questions which must be cleared out of the way.

The first of these concerns the homogeneity of the second
Gospel. The dependence of St. Mark upon an earlier
document, for which the convenient formula ' Q ' may be
adopted, is put forward with special cogency by B. Weiss,
who holds that St. Mark added excerpts from this document to what he recalled of St. Peter's preaching. The
document is held to have contained both Logia and narrative, and, as it was also before the first and third
evangelists, it accounts for those passages in which they
are in agreement against St. Mark. It also offers an
explanation of the appearance of sayings in the second
Gospel. The theory is really a repetition of the theory
of an Ur-Markus, the only difference being that this
oldest source is considered to differ from canonical Mark
by its inclusion of both Narrative and Sayings. The
general objections to the theory of an Ur-Markus will
therefore apply to this, and in addition it may be said
that the agreement of Matthew and Luke against Mark
does not of necessity imply the existence of an earlier
Gospel now lost from which all three drew their material.
It will be shown that where Sayings, properly so called,
are found in the first and third evangelists, they differ so
markedly that it is now generally held that the collection
of Logia before the one was different from that used by
the other, and where they reproduce incidents rather than
discourses it is at least possible that the edition of Mark
which they used differed from that which we have in
canonical Mark. The healing of the centurion's servant may
have been omitted in the later edition which St. Mark
prepared at Rome, though he had included it in his earlier

editions, and it is also most probable that many of these 'agreements' which are found in the non-appearance of personal and picturesque details are to be explained in the same way.

The appearance of sayings in the second Gospel does not present any serious difficulty in this connection. In relating an incident in the life of our Lord, St. Mark would not of necessity be precluded from writing down what Jesus said on the occasion in question. It would be part of the narrative, and without it the account would be pointless and imperfect. That saying might appear in any collection of sayings, as a distinct Logion, separated from its setting, and as such it would find its place in the collection made by St. Luke or by St. Matthew. Its appearance in Mark then would not imply that he had derived it from such a collection. The parable of the Seed growing secretly may here be referred to. It appears only in St. Mark's Gospel, and if it is maintained that he derived it from Q it is very difficult to believe that both St. Matthew and St. Luke by mere coincidence agreed in omitting it. The teaching it conveys would have been peculiarly appropriate at any rate to the disciple of St. Paul, and that he should have omitted it deliberately has never been seriously suggested. Mr. Streeter [1] maintains strongly that St. Mark used Q, but even he admits that his theory breaks down in being applied to this particular parable, and he therefore concludes that St. Mark knew and used Q, ' but only to a limited extent.'

Mr. Streeter adduces, as supporting the theory that St. Mark used Q, the sections describing the Baptism of our Lord and the controversy with reference to the casting out of demons. Both of these sections have been mentioned elsewhere in illustration of the contention that canonical Mark is a later edition of St. Mark's Gospel as first written,

---

[1] *Oxford Studies in the Synoptic Problem*, p. 178.

and to that section of this work we must refer the student.[1]
The abbreviated form, in which the section describing
both the Temptation and the Baptism of our Lord appears
in Mark, is held by Mr. Streeter to show that St. Mark is
epitomising Q. He says that ' An original tradition is
always detailed and picturesque, and would hardly record,
as does St. Mark, a temptation to do nothing in particular.'
But if the Markan record was a reproduction of St. Peter's
preaching, it is certain that it would be conditioned by the
circumstances attending that preaching ; and since we are
told, and have good reason to believe, that St. Peter spoke
as the occasion demanded, the Roman edition might differ
just as the account of the Baptism and Temptation actually
differ in canonical Mark. What was of intense interest
in Palestine or to Jews of the Dispersion in Alexandria
might demand considerable curtailment when prepared
for Christians in Rome.

In the thirteenth chapter of St. Mark's Gospel there
occurs a remarkable section which is known by the name of
the little Apocalypse (Mark xiii. 3-37). It consists apparently of two discourses which have been woven together
to form one whole. The former consists of warnings of
the approaching destruction of Jerusalem, and bears a
close correspondence in style to that class of Jewish
writings which have been called Apocalyptic or Eschatological ; the latter consists of teaching concerning the
Parousia. It appears in all three Gospels, and in all there
is a close verbal correspondence. The record, however, in
the first Gospel is very much closer to that which we find
in Mark. The Lukan record differs mostly in omissions
or abbreviations, except in Luke xxi. 24, which stands
alone and reads like an interpolation reminiscent of
Romans xi. 25. The Matthaean version again reproduces
(chap. xxiv. 19-22) part of the discourse given by our
Lord on sending forth His disciples (chap. x. 17-22), and

[1] See p. 118.

the doublet is characteristic of that Gospel, which often
repeats as part of the Logia that which appears in the
Markan narrative.

Now it is obvious that as part of the Markan narrative
this section is unique. It stands alone in St. Mark's
Gospel as a ' discourse '; it is apocalyptic in construction,
and it lacks that element of moral and spiritual significance
which we find in the parables and other Logia. St. Mark,
as we have seen, does not exhibit that tendency to ' conflation ' which we find in the other evangelists, but in this
section there seems to be an undoubted conflation of
sayings relating to the destruction of Jerusalem, and those
which refer to the Parousia. These facts have given
rise to a number of views concerning the section. Dr.
Stanton considers that it is to be attributed to ' some
Jewish-Christian who was influenced in his general presentation of the distinctively Christian material which he had
at his disposal, by his Jewish conceptions, and amplified
it with expressions familiar to him through Jewish writings.'
If this view be accepted, and to us it seems the most
likely, there is no reason why its author should not be
St. Mark himself. The Pauline as well as the Johannine
writings show that ' Apocalypse ' might characterise the
writings of Christians, and therefore the homogeneity of the
second Gospel need not be destroyed by the appearance of
this original section. Another view is that of Mr. Streeter,
who considers it to be a document dating from the year
70, and revealing, like the rest of St. Mark's Gospel, traces
of Q. We should prefer to say that distinct sayings of
our Lord which appear in the second Gospel also appeared
in the collection of sayings used by St. Matthew. Dr.
Burkitt considers the section to have formed a separate
fly-sheet incorporated into the Gospel by the evangelist,
and the allusion to ' him that readeth,' in Mark xiii. 14,
is cited by him in support. Others again derive the
whole section from Q. It will be observed that these

authorities are agreed in treating the section as a separate document, apocalyptic in character, and incorporated by St. Mark into his Gospel. Attempts to discover its source will necessarily be speculative, and as it is the one section in the Markan narrative which appears to break into the homogeneity of the Gospel, we prefer to regard it as coming from the hand of St. Mark.

The absence of doublets from the second Gospel is perhaps the strongest evidence of its homogeneity. In the first and third Gospels there are many cases in which a saying of our Lord appears more than once. These are fully set forth by Dr. Stanton,[1] and may be studied conveniently in that arrangement. They indicate conclusively that the compilers of those Gospels used more than one source ; and as in nearly every case one of the two sayings occurs in the Markan narrative, the conclusion is inevitable that the doublets are due to the writers combining with Markan narrative, which they used, another source consisting largely, if not entirely, of sayings. This may be seen illustrated in Matthew x. 19–xxiv. 9-14, and also in Luke viii. 17–xii. 2. But when we study the second Gospel from this point of view the case is altogether different. Of the many instances discussed by Dr. Stanton only two are found in Mark.[2] One of these is in the two accounts of feeding the multitude. But it may be urged in reply that scholars are far from agreeing that in this we have two accounts of one miracle, and in our Lord's words recorded in Mark viii. 19, 20 there seems to be a reference to two miracles rather than to one. Rejecting this instance then we find the one instance recorded in Mark ix. 35, Mark x. 41-45, where our Lord rebukes the disciples for their personal ambition to occupy high places in His kingdom. This, says Dr. Wright, is the only instance of a doublet in St. Mark. Even with reference

---

[1] *Op. cit.* p. 54 ff.   [2] Cf. *Oxford Studies*, p. 419.

to this, we may plead that this human weakness in the
disciples may quite easily have shown itself on more than
one occasion, and the phraseology in which our Lord is
represented to have corrected it is by no means identical.
In one case, too, He is said to have reproved them by
bringing a little child into their midst, while in the other
there is no mention of the child.   But even if we accept
this as a true doublet, the single instance should not be
allowed to weigh unduly in considering the homogeneity
of the Gospel.

In passing to a more constructive criticism of the second
Gospel we proceed to consider the history of St. Mark
as that is given us, and such reference to his connection
with the second Gospel as may be discovered in the
writings of the Fathers.

St. Mark was the son of a woman named Mary, and his
mother's home in Jerusalem seems to have been a place of
resort for the disciples.   There is a tradition that the
Upper Room, where the Lord celebrated the last Passover,
as well as the room in which the disciples were assembled
at Pentecost, was in her house.   Some have supposed that
the man carrying a pitcher of water, and the young man
who fled away naked, which are mentioned only in the
Markan narrative, were St. Mark himself.   Papias says
that ' he neither heard the Lord nor followed Him, but
subsequently attached himself to Peter.'   The latter, on
being delivered from prison (Acts xii.), went at once to St.
Mark's house, ' where many were gathered together praying.'
He was well known there and was recognised by the servant,
whose name was inserted in the record by the person
from whom St. Luke derived the earlier chapters of ' The
Acts of the Apostles '—probably from St. Mark himself.
We are told, again by Papias, that St. Mark became the
interpreter of St. Peter, and as the latter was probably
unable to speak Greek with ease, this was likely enough.
It has often been pointed out that the address given by

St. Peter [1] in the house of Cornelius (Acts x. 34 ff.) is an
epitome of the second Gospel, and this becomes significant
if St. Mark was one of the brethren that accompanied
St. Peter from Joppa (Acts x. 23). We have only to
accept that the newly baptized in Caesarea wished to retain
some record of St. Peter's preaching, and that St. Mark
wrote down what St. Peter had said, and left it with them.
Eusebius tells us that St. Mark was sent to Egypt in the
first year of the Emperor Claudius, which would be in
A.D. 41, and both Eusebius and Jerome tell us that he
took his Gospel with him. St. Chrysostom tells us that
he wrote his Gospel in Egypt. Both statements may well
be true if St. Mark, wishing the Church in Alexandria to
possess some record of apostolic teaching on the facts of
Christ's life, re-wrote ' as much as he remembered ' ($\H{o}\sigma\alpha$
$\epsilon\mu\nu\eta\mu\acute{o}\nu\epsilon\upsilon\sigma\epsilon\nu$) of St. Peter's addresses. This document
would pass into the treasured records of the Church in
Alexandria.

We next find St. Mark in the company of Paul and
Barnabas at Antioch. Presumably he had returned from
Egypt to Jerusalem, and accompanied the two apostles
on their missionary journey, which may be assigned to the
year A.D. 50 (Acts xiii. 5). He did not, however, continue
long with them, as he left them at Pamphylia and returned
to Jerusalem. Afterwards he went with Barnabas to
Cyprus, St. Paul having resented his leaving them in
Pamphylia. The strained relations between St. Mark
and St. Paul did not, however, continue long. They were
together when St. Paul wrote his Epistle to the Colossians
(Col. iv. 10), and St. Mark's name occurs again in connection with St. Luke's in the Epistle to Philemon (24).
The reference in the Colossian Epistle shows St. Mark to
be on the point of making a journey from Rome to Asia,
but a few years after this he is again required at Rome by
St. Paul, who says (2 Tim. iv. 11) : ' Take Mark and bring

[1] Zahn, p. 448.

him with thee, for he is profitable to me for the ministry,'
words which Zahn interprets to mean that St. Mark was in
possession of ' treasure of narrative from the lips of Peter
and of other disciples of Jesus, who were accustomed to
come and go in his mother's house.' [1] Apparently he did
return to Rome, for it is generally accepted now that the
reference in 1 Peter v. 13 is to be taken as showing that
St. Mark and St. Peter were together in that city when the
first Epistle of Peter was written. This would be after
the year A.D. 61. This falls in with other references in
Patristic writings. In his *Hypotyposes* Clement of
Alexandria tells us that it was part of the tradition of
former time that ' When Peter had publicly preached the
word in Rome, and declared the Gospel by the Spirit,
those who were present, being many, urged Mark, as one
who had followed him for a long time and remembered
what he said, to record what he stated ; and that he having
made his Gospel gave it to those who made the request
of him ; and that Peter was careful neither to hinder him
nor to encourage him in the work.' [2] Zahn contrasts the
last clause in this quotation from the *Hypotyposes* with a
statement made by Eusebius (ii. 15) to the effect that St.
Peter was pleased with the zeal of St. Mark, and that his
work obtained the sanction of his authority for the purpose
of being used in the churches. Zahn reconciles the two
statements by explaining that St. Peter took no part in
the transactions that led up to St. Mark's undertaking this
work, but when the work was completed, accepted it, and
approved of it. The last Father to be cited in this connection is Irenaeus, who says (*Haer.* iii. 11) that ' Matthew
published his Gospel . . . while Peter and Paul were
preaching and founding the Church in Rome. After their
departure Mark, the disciple and interpreter of Peter,
himself also has handed down to us in writing the things
which were preached by Peter.'

[1] Zahn, vol. ii. p. 430.   [2] *Ibid.* p. 432.

The patristic testimony fits in fairly well with such an outline of St. Mark's connection with St. Peter as is given us in the Scriptures. The statements made by the different Fathers, however, reveal one detail at least in which there seems to be some contradiction. Some of them connect St. Mark's Gospel with Egypt, while others declare that it was produced in Rome. It is probably because of this uncertainty that more emphasis is not laid upon patristic testimony in discussing the origins of the Markan Gospel. But we have only to suppose, what bears every mark of probability, that St. Mark wrote down what he remembered of St. Peter's preaching both while he superintended the Church in Alexandria and later on when he was again associated with St. Peter in Rome, to see that the apparent contradiction between the Fathers may be resolved. Chrysostom and Jerome are right in ascribing the Gospel to Egypt, and Clement is equally right in declaring Rome to be its birthplace. We shall show presently that the Markan narrative in the first Gospel bears unmistakable marks of an Alexandrian origin, while canonical Mark as distinctly points to Rome. But if these marks appear in these two Gospels, the Lukan Mark has many traits which indicate a Palestinian origin, and there is no reason why St. Mark should not have written an even earlier edition of his Gospel which was left at Caesarea, where it would pass into the hands of St. Luke when he visited that town.

The theory of three Markan editions has been strongly advocated in England by Dr. Arthur Wright, who claims that it has all the advantages without any of the improbability of an Ur-Markus. He holds that the first edition is to be found in St. Luke's Gospel, embedded in other matter, the first Gospel contains the second, and the second Gospel the third. Unfortunately for its acceptance Dr. Wright's masterly analysis of these three editions which he names Proto,- Deutero,- and Trito-Mark has scarcely had the justice done to it which it deserves, and this is largely due to the fact that he has woven this theory into that which assumes an oral basis as underlying all three, the oral basis having taken many years to form. As we have shown, there are good reasons for rejecting the theory of an oral tradition as basis for these Gospels, but, if this part of Dr. Wright's contention be removed, we hold that he has carried the analysis of the Synoptic Gospels a long way towards a conclusion. The characteristics of the Proto- and Deutero-Mark will be considered in discussing the salient features of the first and third Gospels. We shall here content ourselves with noticing features of the second Gospel, which show it to be secondary to those Gospels where the three have a common narrative.

The references to the Baptist in this Gospel are such as indicate a later production for a Gentile, or largely Gentile, Church, such as existed in Rome, with which Mark's Gospel, as we have seen, was associated from a very early date. To such a Church the interest in the Baptist would be slight. It would be quite otherwise to a Church which belonged to Palestine, or whose members were Jews of the Dispersion. We know from the fourth Gospel how great was the interest aroused by the Forerunner, and we can easily understand that his preaching and his contact with the Messiah would call for somewhat detailed treatment. It would not, however, be so in Rome a whole generation after the death of the Baptist, and thus we find that such references to him as appear in the second Gospel are, in comparison with what we have in the other two, very slight. They constitute a mere outline of his relation to Christ ; just enough to serve as an introduction to the Gospel. Even thus the record is not without those vivid touches which make the second Gospel the most dramatic of the three, and the one most full of those personal reminiscences which have done so much to make the Person of our Lord stand out before the devout imagination of succeeding ages. These appear in the statements that the heavens were rent asunder at the Baptism, and that during the Temptation—an event always closely connected with the Baptism—our Lord was in the haunt of wild beasts.

The vivid touches of the second Gospel we consider to be distinctly secondary features. Their non-appearance in the other Synoptic Gospels is generally accounted for on the ground of editorial omissions by the respective editors. The reasons assigned for such action on the part of the editors are twofold. Many words and phrases are held to have been rejected as being pictorial and contributing nothing of real value to the history. By editors who had other matter which they deemed of importance, and who were pressed for space, these would be at once surrendered. But against this it may be urged that the writings reveal no such tendency as we should expect in a modern writer compiling a history, and careful to introduce nothing which did not bear immediately upon the point with which he was dealing. There is a personal, affectionate note in all three evangelists which would lead them, and has led them, to admit matter which was of no distinct historical value, but which they included because of the reverence which they felt for all details of the wonderful story. The principle of economy, too, does not appear in other parts of their work. They admit phrases and even whole clauses which we should imagine they might have excluded without loss. Their whole attitude towards their sources is rather that of almost scrupulous fidelity than that of arbitrary rejection of matter which to them seemed without value. Finally, while it might be possible for one or other of the first and third evangelists to omit such matter as unimportant, it is very difficult to believe that they should have, by an extraordinary coincidence, agreed upon what should be omitted and what retained. Most

of the phrases under consideration are lacking from both
the first and third evangelists. They wrote for very
different readers, at different times, and in different places,
and yet we are asked to believe that they fastened upon
identical words and phrases for excision. They include
the ' awkward parenthesis ' of Mark ii. 10, but agree to
omit the statement that Jesus took the little children into
His arms when He blessed them. If, however, these
features of the second Gospel were secondary, their non-
appearance in the other two is easily explained. They
do not appear because they were not found in the edition
of Mark which they used. It is sometimes urged that the
fuller statement is always the earlier, and that the existence
of such picturesque details in the second Gospel indicates
priority. But this contention ignores the circumstances
in which the Gospels were written. Those who hold this
view are unconsciously imagining that the works were
produced under modern conditions which govern the
production of literature, whereas this Markan narrative
reveals everywhere traits which bear out the old tradition
that it was but the transcript of the preaching of St. Peter,
and that he told the story not according to some distinct
plan in his own mind, but just as the circumstance and
need of his hearers might demand. The whole narrative
is a record of apostolic preaching. As such, we contend,
the story which was told last would be the fullest and
most detailed of all. The preacher would discover as he
went on what details were of most interest to his hearers.
Incidents upon which he dwelt at first might be omitted
on subsequent occasions ; or St. Mark, in writing down the
story for others than those for whom he wrote at first,
might omit one incident and insert another which had
not found a place in the earliest writing. But always,
in response to the craving of those to whom the personal
life of Jesus was a matter of supreme interest and importance, the story, either as given by St. Peter, or written

down by St. Mark, would reveal in its latest edition features
which would make it vivid, dramatic, and full of that
' atmosphere ' which we may be sure our Lord carried
with Him wherever He went.

Another reason assigned for the omission of such details
is that the first and third evangelists would be careful to
omit anything which seemed to be derogatory to the
person of Christ or to the character of the apostles. It
is not shown why this should have been less safeguarded
by St. Mark than by the others. Even if canonical Mark
was prior to Matthew, it could not have been so by more
than a few years, and a tendency which appears in one
writing might have been expected in the other, since both
would reflect the feeling of the same age. But putting
this consideration on one side, we would urge in reply that
the insertion of these personal details can scarcely be said
to lower the dignity of our Lord and His disciples. The
character of Christ is far from being compromised by the
statement that when He looked upon the rich young ruler
He loved him, yet this detail is omitted from both the
first and the third Gospel. In another passage we read
that Christ was grieved for the hardness of men's hearts ;
this does not appear in the first or in the third evangelist,
and its non-appearance in these Gospels is generally explained on the lines stated above, but it is to be questioned
whether the statement shows as much of the sternness of
Christ's indignation as is evidenced in the great denunciation of the Scribes and Pharisees given by St. Matthew.[1]
If any passage would seem to reveal Christ in a condition
which, for want of understanding, might be held to be
one of weakness, it is that which describes Him in the
garden of Gethsemane praying that the cup might pass
from Him, and acknowledging the weakness of the flesh.
The disciples certainly appear in what may be called a
compromising position on that occasion. Yet the incident

[1] Cf. Mark viii. 33=Matt. xvi. 23.

is recorded by all three evangelists. These omissions of course belong to the same group of characteristics which find an extreme example in what has been called the great omission of St. Luke, and this will be fully considered in discussing the Markan sections of the third Gospel in chapter vi.

The use of the word εὐαγγέλιον is full of significance in a study of the Markan narrative in the three Gospels. In canonical Mark the word occurs with considerable frequency and is used in an absolute sense (Mark i. 14, 15, viii. 35, x. 29). It does not occur at all in St. Luke. Used absolutely it is absent from St. Matthew, and in the parallels cited above it does not appear at all. This is the more extraordinary because St. Luke uses the verb εὐαγγελίζομαι frequently (iv. 18, vii. 22, viii. 1, xvi. 16), and as the follower of St. Paul he would be familiar with the marked use of the noun by that apostle. The editor of the first Gospel has no objection to the word itself ; he uses it in combination with other terms (lx. 35, xxvi. 13). There does not seem to be any reason why he should not retain the word in passages borrowed from the source which presumably he was using. Few facts better illustrate the value of the three editions theory than does this. The Christian Church was slow to recognise the necessity for any formulated or canonical presentation of the Gospel story. St. Peter gave his account of the wonderful life, ' in accordance with the needs of his hearers.' It was only after it had become evident that the return of the Lord in Messianic glory would not be as immediate as the Church had thought, and when meanwhile the attempts to seduce the Gentile converts from the faith made it necessary that they should have some assurance of the certainty of those things in which they had been instructed ; it was only then that the necessity for a guaranteed account of Christ's words and works began to be felt. Thus we find St. Paul speaking of the presentation of certain facts

as being ' in accordance with my Gospel,' and of the
necessity of prophesying ' according to the analogy of the
faith ' (Rom. xii. 6), and he exhorts Timothy to ' hold fast
the pattern of sound words which thou hast heard from
me ' (2 Tim. i. 13). This resolving of experience into
historical statement is well illustrated by the use of πίστις
in the New Testament. This word has a whole gamut
of uses in which we can detect its passing from a wholly
subjective relationship to Christ into the description of a
more objective ' Faith,' a formulary or creed ' once delivered
to the saints ' (Jude 3). If, as seems likely, the Lukan
edition of the Markan narrative was the earliest, we
should expect to find the word εὐαγγέλιον scarcely used
at all. In the later edition, embodied in the first Gospel,
the word would begin to appear, while in trito-Mark or
our Canonical Gospel—written later in Rome—where St.
Paul's influence would be added to St. Peter's, the word
would be fully established, and this is precisely what we
do find. It is to be noticed that in the first Epistle of
Peter (iv. 17) the word εὐαγγέλιον appears used in an
objective sense as connoting a body of authoritative
doctrine to which obedience was expected, and if this
Epistle was written when St. Mark had rejoined St. Peter
in Rome (1 Peter v. 13) the appearance of the word in the
trito-Mark becomes all the more significant. Dr. Stanton
calls attention to the appearance of the word in an absolute
use in canonical Mark, but draws the conclusion that it is
due to the alteration of some reviser of the original.
Unless positive proof for this can be adduced, it seems better
to accept the explanation given above.

The secondary character of canonical Mark is further
illustrated from the appearance within it of Pauline
features. In the second Gospel the death of Christ is
emphasised in a way which is very marked when passages
are compared with their parallels in the other two Gospels,
and in one passage (x. 45) we have the much discussed

sentence ' The Son of Man is come . . . to give His life
a ransom for many.' The word λύτρον occurs only in
this passage in the New Testament, but its derivative
ἀπολύτρωσις is frequent in St. Paul's letters. Now if
St. Luke had canonical Mark before him when he compiled
his Gospel, on what principle did he omit this passage ?
His teacher, St. Paul, had made this view of a mediatorial
death the prominent feature of his teaching. Why should
St. Luke fix upon this expression of all others for omission ?
Nor do we find much relief from our perplexity when we
are told that the passage is not an omission of St. Luke's,
but ' belongs to a later recension of the Markan text.'
For it is found word for word in the first Gospel, and if
this explanation be accepted we should have to suppose
that the recension took place subsequently to St. Luke's
use of Mark, but before the first evangelist had incorporated
the Markan narrative in his Gospel. It is no safe conclusion
which is based upon such finessing.

Dr. Stanton rightly observes that in the emphasis laid
upon the mediatorial aspect of Christ's death, there is
nothing that is distinctively and peculiarly Pauline. St.
Peter also urges the significance of our Lord's death when
he says ' ye were redeemed . . . with the precious blood
as of a lamb without blemish and without spot, even the
blood of Christ ' (1 Peter i. 19). The appearance of this
saying of our Lord in the later editions may thus be a
Petrine, and not a Pauline, note. At the same time St.
Mark's association with St. Paul both during the short
time when he accompanied him on his missionary journey,
and later on when he was again associated with him in
Rome, may have led him to see a significance in certain
sayings of Christ as given by St. Peter, which had not
impressed his thought and imagination when he first
wrote down his memoirs of the preaching of that apostle.
In any case the emphasis, whether made by St. Peter or
by St. Mark, belongs to a later period of apostolic teaching.

In St. Peter's speeches recorded in the Acts of the Apostles, he dwells upon *the fact* of Christ's death ; *the interpretation* of that death belongs to a later stage ; and even if we had not the significant passage quoted from the Epistle to guide us, we might have felt sure that it would be reflected in the teaching of St. Peter, especially when he had to declare the value of that death to Gentiles. We conclude then that the words are absent from the third Gospel because they did not appear in the edition of Mark which St. Luke used, and they have their place in the later editions because the emphasis they carry belongs to a later period in the public ministry of the apostles.

If we turn to the eschatological passages of the three Gospels the same feature of change of expression due to different circumstances appears. Let us take a single example. The declaration of Christ concerning His Messianic reign made before the council of the chief priests is given in all three Gospels (Mark xiv. 62, Matt. xxvi. 64, Luke xxii. 69), but with significant alterations. As Dr. Stanton points out, the original form of Mark is best preserved in the first Gospel. The alterations in Luke are evidently editorial corrections made so as to emphasise the fact of Christ's *Messianic position* being given to Him immediately, whereas the record in Matthew declares that He would immediately *appear*. In the later edition, however, preserved for us in canonical Mark, the Church had come to see that the Parousia would not be immediate, and the words ἀπ' ἄρτι are in consequence omitted. Now if canonical Mark was the source from which the later evangelists drew their account of this declaration, they must have added the words indicating an immediate manifestation ; and that they should do so when every day made the Parousia, which they expected, further removed from the time when the words were first spoken, is inexplicable. Dr. Stanton speaks of the significant alteration in canonical Mark as being made by the ' last reviser of Mark,' and we have no objection to that phrase except that we hold that St. Mark was his own reviser.

Another strongly corroborative indication of the secondary character of canonical Mark is mentioned by Dr. E. A. Abbott (Art. ' Gospels,' *Enc. Biblica*).[1] It is that in the second Gospel we have a great many names inserted which are lacking from the parallels in the other two Gospels. Dr. Abbott points out that the tendency to insert names of persons is most marked in Apocryphal Gospels, and their presence in the second Gospel indicates a late writer. If then the editors of the first and third Gospels had these names before them in their source, but chose to omit them, they were acting contrary to the common tendency. It is better to suppose that the names were not included in the earlier editions of Mark, but that in an edition prepared much later, and so far away from the scene of the incidents recorded as Rome, the names would be inserted naturally. Every missionary knows that to mention the names of converts in published accounts of their work among a people hostile to Christianity is fraught with peril to those who are mentioned. Such names are therefore excluded from editions published where the identification of individuals would be easy, but appear in the trito-Mark. The difficult question of the appearance in the fourth Gospel of the raising of Lazarus finds its best explanation in an application of this rule. We know that there were attempts made to put Lazarus also to death, and other members of the family at Bethany seem to have been threatened. At any rate, although the Synoptists record the saying of Christ that the name of the woman who broke the bottle of spikenard and with its contents anointed the feet of Jesus, should be mentioned wherever the Gospel was proclaimed, that name was never

Omitting the name ' Jesus,' there are seventy-three names in Mark as against twenty-seven in Matt. and twenty-two in Luke.

mentioned by them. It was left for the author of the
fourth Gospel long years afterwards, when probably both
Lazarus and Mary were dead, to introduce the story of
the raising of Lazarus, and of Mary's expression of grateful
love. We shall therefore find an easy explanation of the
appearance of names in the canonical Mark. One example
of this usage may be specially referred to. We read in
canonical Mark that the Simon who carried the cross of
our Lord was ' the father of Alexander and Rufus,' a
reference which in the way it is introduced in the second
Gospel seems pointless. But when we return to the list
of the names of those to whom St. Paul sent greeting when
he wrote the Epistle to the Romans we find that one of
those mentioned is Rufus. Now ' Rufus ' is by no means
an uncommon name, but if the surmise is correct that the
man to whom St. Paul refers was the son of Simon of
Cyrene, then the insertion of the name in the Roman
edition of St. Mark's writings ceases to be abrupt. The
reference would at once be picked up by Roman Christians.
So again the name of Pilate (Mark xv. 1, Matt. xxvii. 2,
Luke xxiii. 1) in the Caesarean edition and in the Roman
is introduced without explanation of the position of the
man named. Persons living either in Caesarea or in
Rome did not need information as to Pilate's position,
but in the edition prepared for Jews living in Alexandria
the words are added which informed the reader that Pilate
was ' the Governor.'

Geographical names have a similarly marked use. The
story, for instance, of the deliverance of ' Legion ' from
the demons is given in all three Gospels, but a well-known
difficulty, clearly marked in the uncertainties of the text
in the passages, arises from the fact that different names
are given in all three. Accepting the best supported text
in each case we find that in the first Gospel we have ' the
district of the Gadarenes,' in the second ' the district of
the Gerasenes,' and in the third ' the district of the

Gergesenes.' There has been much discussion arising out
of this difference, but the best explanation we have seen
is one which is based upon the theory of three editions of
Mark, in which the Palestinian edition gives the name
of the town accurately as ' Gergesa,' the Egyptian edition
gives the name ' Gadara,' which was better known abroad,
while the Roman edition gives the official name of the
district, which was ' Gerasa.'

The Latinisms of the second Gospel are frequent enough
to attract attention, and they have generally been cited
in support of the Roman origin of the Gospel. Nothing
decisive can be inferred from the use of these words (a
list of which is given in the article on the Gospel of St.
Mark by Dr. S. D. F. Salmond in Hastings' *Bible Dictionary*),
because they are just such words as an editor would be
justified in altering if he saw fit to do so, and again they are
for the most part words which would rapidly come into
use in outlying parts of the Roman Empire, so that if they
were in the first edition of the Markan narrative they
might or might not be changed by an editor. They are,
however, far more frequent in the second Gospel than
in the others, and to this extent they support the Roman
origin of the canonical Mark. One or two changes, too,
seem significant. Thus in Luke xx. 22 the regular word
for ' tax ' is used, but in both the Egyptian and Roman
editions we have κῆνσος, the Latin ' Census.' In Mark
xv. 39 the Graecised form of the Latin ' Centurion ' is used,
but in the other editions this appears in the form ἑκατοντ-
άρχης. More significant perhaps is the passage in Mark xii. 42
where St. Mark gives us the value in Roman coinage of
δύο λεπτά, ' two mites,' which, he says, make a κοδράντης,
Latin Quadrans. St. Luke mentions the δύο λεπτά, but
does not give their Roman value, the term being easily
understood in an edition prepared for use in Palestine.
In recording the cure of the paralytic the evangelists use
a different word in each case for ' bed.' In the first Gospel

the usual word for bed is used (κλίνη), in the third St.
Luke uses the word usually employed by physicians for
a sick-bed (κλινίδιον), but in the second Gospel, as we
have it, the word κράββατος, the Graecised form of the
word used for a soldier's wallet, appears. Other similar
words are ξέστης (Mark vii. 4) and σπεκουλάτωρ (Mark
vi. 27) which appear in the trito-Mark alone. The
easily recognised 'Praetorium' appears in both the
Egyptian and the Roman edition, but the way in which it
is introduced in the latter as a closer definition of the
indefinite αὐλή indicates again the Roman edition in
canonical Mark.

The date of the composition of the second Gospel has
been given variously from the earliest time, and this
uncertainty seems to be due to a failure to distinguish
between canonical Mark and earlier editions of the same
work. The Paschal Chronicle places it as early as A.D. 40,
and Eusebius assigns it to the third year of Claudius
(A.D. 43). Others again, like Irenaeus and Clement of
Alexandria, say that it was written after St. Peter's arrival
at Rome (A.D. 63). But these are not agreed, for Clement
speaks of the Gospel as being in existence during Peter's
lifetime, while Irenaeus says that it was written ' after his
departure.' This conflict of statement is probably due to
the fact that the different authorities had different editions
before them when they wrote. Modern scholars are fairly
agreed in assigning canonical Mark, for an approximate
date, to the period between A.D. 65 and 70. In the
Oxford Studies, however, we find the Rev. W. E. Addis
asserting that the Gospel was written subsequently to the
destruction of Jerusalem. The same view is held by
P. W. Schmiedel.

ADDITIONAL NOTE I

ANALYSIS OF THE SECOND GOSPEL WITH NOTES

Chap. i. 1-8. *The Ministry of John the Baptist.*

      9-13. *The Baptism and Temptation of Jesus.*

    14-22. *Jesus returns to Galilee, and teaches in Caper-*
          naum.

    23-45. *Works of Healing.*

i. 1. The word ἀρχή reads suspiciously like an interpolation
from a Lectionary, and it is absent from one Syriac
version, but see Swete *in loco*. υἱοῦ τοῦ θεοῦ. See
Wright, *Synopsis*.

  2. The quotation from Malachi was added in trito-Mark as
the idea of the Fore-runner became established in the
Christian Church, without alteration of ἐν τῷ Ἡσαίᾳ
which appeared in the earlier editions.

  4. Cf. Acts i. 22. ἀρξάμενος ἀπὸ τοῦ βαπτίσματος Ἰωάνου.
The phrase throws light upon St. Luke's source for the
early chapters of Acts, and upon St. Mark's plan in the
composition of his Gospel.

  5-6. Not found in the proto-Mark used by St. Luke. Note
that John's condemnation of the different Jewish sects
is not found in canonical Mark, as it would be inapposite
in a gospel prepared for Roman Christians.

  8. καὶ πυρί. Omitted from trito-Mark ; see page 81. The
reference to the winnowing work of the Messiah is also
omitted.

  9. John's self-depreciation in the presence of the Messiah
would be of importance to Jewish Christians. It is
therefore included in deutero-Mark, but omitted from
the other editions.

  10. σχιζομένους. A vivid detail peculiar to trito-Mark. See p. 79.
Another similar detail is found in ἦν μετὰ τῶν θηρίων.
The descent of the Spirit upon our Lord is described in
practically the same terms in each edition. This makes
the points of difference all the more significant. The
Temptation is given in outline in trito-Mark.

i. 20. μετὰ τῶν μισθωτῶν. A detail peculiar to trito-Mark. The call of the four disciples is not given in proto-Mark. In that edition St. Mark records the later and more definite call. (Luke v. 1-11.) ἀμφιβάλλοντας. See Swete *in loco*.

23-28. The cure of the demoniac is not given in deutero-Mark. Note the close verbal resemblance between proto- and trito-Mark. It is difficult to see why this incident should have been omitted from the first Gospel if the editor used canonical Mark.

33. Vivid details peculiar to trito-Mark.

41. σπλαγχνισθείς. Another detail peculiar to trito-Mark. See p. 119.

44. Proto- and trito-Mark have προσένεγκε περὶ τοῦ καθαρισμοῦ σου. But in deutero-Mark we read τὸ δῶρον, this simple expression requiring no explanation for Jewish Christians.

Chap. ii. 1-12. *Jesus cures a paralytic.*
13-22. *The feast in Matthew's house.*
23-28. *Discussion on the keeping of the Sabbath.*

ii. 2. A vivid detail peculiar to trito-Mark.

4. κράβαττον. Luke has κλινίδιον ; Matthew, κλίνη. For κράβαττος—the Greek form of Grabatus—see Swete *in loco*. Its appearance in trito-Mark is an indication of Rome as the birthplace of the second Gospel.

10. For the 'awkward parenthesis,' see page 120.

17. Matthew contains the quotation ἔλεος θέλω καὶ οὐ θυσίαν —a passage frequently on the lips of our Lord. See Matt. ix. 13, xii. 7.

22. In proto-Mark we have the significant addition καὶ οὐδεὶς πιὼν παλαιὸν θέλει νέον· λέγει γάρ· ὁ παλαιὸς χρηστός ἐστιν. See Hort, *Judaistic Christianity*, pp. 23 ff.

26. ἐπὶ Ἀβιάθαρ ἀρχιερέως. This does not appear in proto- and deutero-Mark. 'It was omitted on account of the historical difficulty.' Hawkins, *Horae Synopticae*, p. 99. It may, however, have been an addition made in the third edition. 'It may have been an editorial note.' Swete *in loco*. See also Wright, *Synopsis*, p. 25, and

Stanton, *The Gospels as Historical Documents*, vol. ii.
p. 145.

ii. 27. An addition in trito-Mark. No explanation of the
verse as an omission from proto- and deutero-Mark is
satisfactory. See page 84. In deutero-Mark we have an
addition bearing on the relation of the priesthood to the
Law, concluding with the words τοῦ ἱεροῦ μεῖζόν ἐστιν ὧδε.
Such a statement would be full of meaning to Jewish
Christians: the words are therefore included in an
edition intended for their use, and need not be relegated
to Q.

Chap. iii. 1-6. *Jesus cures a man with a withered hand.*
7-19. *Jesus continues His Ministry and appoints*
twelve Apostles.
20-30. *Discussion on Mighty Works.*
31-35. *The true ' Brethren' of Jesus.*

iii. 5. περιβλεψάμενος αὐτοὺς μετ' ὀργῆς συλλυπούμενος ἐπὶ
τῇ πωρώσει τῆς καρδίας αὐτῶν. An addition in trito-
Mark rather than an omission made by Matthew and
Luke. See page 121.

6. μετὰ τῶν Ἡρωδιανῶν. See Swete *in loco.*

17. Note the translation of βοανηργές—necessary for Roman
Christians. The clause οὓς καὶ ἀποστόλους ὠνόμασεν
peculiar to the third Gospel may be an editorial addition.
The cure of the Centurion's servant given in proto-and
deutero-Mark does not appear in trito-Mark. See p. 106.
Our Lord's testimony concerning the Baptist is also
omitted. See p. 118.

20-35. The controversy between our Lord and the Pharisees
as to His dependence on Beelzebub for the power to
perform miracles is not from Q, or there would be
greater similarity in language. See p. 84. The two
verses in Matt. xii. 27-28 are omitted from the trito-
Mark as having greater significance for Jewish Christians
than for Roman readers.

30. ἔνοχος ἔσται αἰωνίου ἁμαρτήματος. See Swete and other
Commentators.

31. ἔρχεται. Note the vivid historic present.

Chap. iv. 1-34. *Teaching by parables.*
  35-41. *Jesus stills a storm.*
 v. 1-20. *The cure of the Gadarene demoniac.*
  21-43. *Jesus cures the woman with the issue of blood,
   and raises the daughter of Jairus.*

iv. 1-34. This section consists of Parables with connective
matter in vv. 10-12. That this section consists of the
teaching of Jesus rather than a narrative of His doings
does not necessarily denote that its origin is to be found
in Q. There was no reason why Peter should not refer
to Christ's teaching in the course of his preaching. If
the whole section was derived from Q, it is difficult to
account for the fact that the parable of the Seed growing
secretly is not given by St. Matthew, and that the
parable of the Leaven is omitted by St. Mark.

 26-29. Peculiar to the second gospel. For a good interpretation of this parable, see commentary by Gould in
the *I.C.C. Series.*

 35-37. Note the historic presents.

 39. σιώπα, πεφίμωσο. Vivid touches peculiar to Mark.

v. 1. Γερασηνῶν. See above, p. 127. Compare Wright, *Synopsis
in loco.*

 3-5. A vivid addition in trito-Mark. The account of this
incident is much abbreviated in deutero-Mark.

 15. ἱματισμένον, a word which occurs nowhere else in New
Testament. St. Luke retains the ἅπαξ λεγόμενον, a
fact difficult to explain except on the ground of fidelity
to a document.

 30. An interpretation of the personal consciousness of Jesus
peculiar to trito-Mark. Cf. Luke viii. 46.

 41. ταλιθὰ, κοῦμι. Note the translation of the Aramaic—a
necessity to Roman Christians. The remarkable fulness
of detail in this section indicates its Petrine origin.

Chap. vi. 1-6. *Jesus teaches in the Synagogue.*
  7-13. *The Mission of the Twelve Disciples.*
  14-29. *The death of John the Baptist.*

vi. 3. ὁ τέκτων ὁ υἱὸς τῆς Μαρίας. The corresponding phrase
in deutero-Mark is ὁ τοῦ τέκτονος υἱός. If canonical

Mark was before the editor of the first Gospel then this
term cannot be reconciled with the tendency to enhance
the supernatural view of our Lord which is brought
forward to account for features of the first Gospel. If,
however, canonical Mark is a later edition, the difference
can be accounted for on the ground that the doctrine of
the Virgin Birth had been accepted by the Church when
the Roman edition was prepared by St. Mark.

vi. 13. ἤλειφον ἐλαίῳ. An addition in the third edition. Cf.
Mayor on James v. 14.

14. ὁ βασιλεὺς Ἡρώδης. Cf. Luke xix. 12. Herod's mission
to Rome to seek the title of 'King' would be known in
that city, and it therefore appears in the Roman edition.
The part played by Herodias in the death of John was
not included in proto-Mark, a sufficient reference having
been made in Luke iii. 19.

27. σπεκουλάτωρ. An obvious Latinism which appears
appropriately in the Roman edition. See Swete *in loco*.

Chap. vi. 30-44. *Jesus feeds the five thousand.*
45-52. *Jesus walks on the sea.*
53-56. *Jesus cures the sick in Gennesaret.*

vi. 34. ἐσπλαγχνίσθη. A vivid touch in the third edition.

39. συμπόσια συμπόσια. See Blass, *Gr.* p. 145. The phrases
in Luke and Matthew are κατακλίνατε αὐτοὺς κλισίας
and ἀνακλιθῆναι respectively. These may be editorial
emendations of what is generally considered to be a
Semitic construction. See, however, Moulton's *Prolegomena*, p. 97. ἐπὶ τῷ χλωρῷ χόρτῳ. Cf. John
vi. 10.

40. πρασιαὶ πρασιαί. See p. 119, and Gould and Swete *in
loco*.

45-52. Omitted in proto-Mark. Peter's attempt to walk on
the water appears only in deutero-Mark. It is difficult
to see whence the evangelist derived it, if he was
dependent on canonical Mark. Its omission from the
latter would be casual.

53. προσωρμίσθησαν. A vivid detail.

vii. 1. At this point in the Markan narrative occurs 'the great omission' in St. Luke's Gospel. See p. 155.

2. These verses peculiar to the second gospel give exactly the explanation which would be necessary to Roman readers. They would not be necessary for Jewish Christians in Alexandria, and accordingly they are not found in the deutero-Mark.

11. κορβᾶν, note again the translation of the Aramaic word. Note also that the severity of the strictures against the Pharisees are modified in trito-Mark. See p. 71.

19. καθαρίζων πάντα τὰ βρώματα. See Field, *Notes on the Translation of the New Testament*, pp. 31, 32, and compare Acts x. 15.

24. The clauses peculiar to St. Mark in this verse illustrate again the vivid detail of trito-Mark, and indicate the eye-witness—St. Peter.

25. Ἑλληνίς Συροφονίκισσα τῷ γένει. See Swete *in loco*, and above p. 155.

32-37. Peculiar to trito-Mark. It is difficult to see why this incident should have been omitted from the first Gospel if canonical Mark was before the editor.

34. ἐφφαθά. Again the Aramaic word is translated.

viii. 10. Δαλμανουθά. In *Matthew* we have Μαγαδάν. See Swete *in loco* and Hastings, *D. B.*, *sub. verb.* 'Magada.'

11-21. Here again the strictures pronounced against the Pharisees are less severe than in Matthew. Also the sign of Jona, which does not appear in trito-Mark, is given without explanation in deutero-Mark.

22-26. This section is peculiar to trito-Mark. Again we may ask why it should be omitted from Matthew, if the editor used canonical Mark.

viii. 27-29. The commendation of St. Peter is not given in trito-
Mark.

    33. We may ask why our Lord's severe rebuke to St. Peter
should appear in Matthew, if the 'tendency' of that
Gospel was to shield the reputation of the disciples.
See p. 121.

    35. καὶ τοῦ εὐαγγελίου. See p. 122.

Chap. ix. 1-28. *The Transfiguration and the cure of a demoniac boy.*

          29-32. *Second announcement of the Passion.*

          33-50. *Discussion on true greatness, toleration, and
offences.*

ix. 1-13. In the Lukan parallel (chap. ix.), three verses (31-33)
are peculiar to that Gospel. It is difficult to see how
St. Luke could have inserted in this narrative a scrap of
this sort taken from some external source. If it was in
the Markan edition which he used, this difficulty is
removed.

    11-13. Here we have verses which do not appear in Luke,
and the 'omission' is as difficult to explain as the
'insertion' mentioned in the preceding note.

    15. ἰδόντες αὐτὸν ἐξεθαμβήθησαν. A vivid addition in
trito-Mark.

    19. ἄπιστος καὶ διεστραμμένη. So in proto- and deutero-
Mark. The words καὶ διεστραμμένη are omitted in
trito-Mark. See p. 121.

    21-25. Another vivid detail in trito-Mark. The differences
in the three accounts of this section are easily accounted
for on the theory of three editions.

    30. οὐκ ἤθελεν ἵνα τις γνοῖ. An addition in trito-Mark.
Its non-appearance in Matthew and Luke cannot be
explained as due to abbreviation for want of space,
since there would be no great gain.

    31. The details of our Lord's death and resurrection do not
appear in the third Gospel. Is it conceivable that Luke
would have omitted them if he had used canonical
Mark ?

    33. In the Matthaean Mark we have here the incident of the
paying of tribute money. This can scarcely be assigned

to Q.   See *Oxford Studies in Syn. Problem*, p. 137.
Note in the Matthaean record the use of the phrases
τὰ δίδραχμα, and οὐ τελεῖ δίδραχμα.

ix. 36.   ἐναγκαλισάμενος αὐτό.   A vivid touch (cf. x. 16).

38-41.   This section does not appear in deutero-Mark.

43-48.   St. Luke did not find this section in the proto-Mark;
it therefore does not appear in the third Gospel.

44-50.   These verses have their counterpart in the collections
of sayings used by St. Matthew and St. Luke.   They
appear in the Markan narrative as a feature of the
trito-Mark.

Chap. x.   1-12.   *A discourse on divorce.*

13-22.   *Little children and the rich young ruler.*

23-31.   *A discourse on riches and rewards.*

32-45.   *Third announcement of the Passion.   Zebedee's
sons.*

46-52.   *The healing of Bartimæus.*

x. 1-12.   This section does not appear in proto-Mark.   In the
Roman edition divorce is forbidden in absolute terms,
but in deutero-Mark, intended, we must remember, for
Jewish Christians, an exception is made in cases of open
adultery (πορνεία).   The Jewish 'tendency' of the first
Gospel is thus fully maintained.

14.   ἠγανάκτησεν and ἐναγκαλισάμενος (16) are vivid touches
peculiar to trito-Mark.   So also is προσδραμών, v. 17.

18.   τί με λέγεις ἀγαθόν; Here Luke and Mark are in agreement.   The different form which appears in Matthew
τί με ἐρωτᾶς περὶ τοῦ ἀγαθοῦ ; may be an editorial alteration.   But see Gould and Swete *in loco*.   The alteration
is not so great as at first sight appears, for in trito-Mark
the emphasis is not on the pronoun με, but on ἀγαθόν,
and the fuller statement of Matthew is implied in Mark.

21-22.   ἐμβλέψας ἠγάπησεν and στυγνάσας are further illustrations of the vividness of trito-Mark.   No reason appears
why the editors of the first and third Gospels should
have omitted these words.   See p. 119.

25.   τρυμάλια.   This appears in proto-Mark as τρῆμα, and in
deutero-Mark as τρυπήμα.   The difference may be
explained on editorial grounds.   The Lukan word τρῆμα,

as well as βελόνη, which follows, is a medical term (see
Hobart, *The Medical Language of St. Luke*, p. 60), and
τρυμάλια is a late and rare word.

x. 29. In the corresponding verse in deutero-Mark we have a
considerable enlargement of this, and the added words
are in agreement with the Jewish 'tendency' of which
we have had so many examples in the first Gospel.
τοῦ εὐαγγελίου. See p. 122.

32. Note the extraordinary vividness of this verse, and compare Matthew xx. 17 and Luke xix. 28.

34. ἀποκτενοῦσιν. This is the word used in proto- and in
trito-Mark. In deutero-Mark we have σταυρῶσαι.
There is no need to suppose that this was an alteration
made by the editor reflecting the actual event. As
Gould points out, the scourging implied crucifixion, and
St. Mark may have used one work in the first edition
and the other word in the second.

35-40. This section is omitted in proto-Mark. If it be held
that St. Luke purposely omitted it to save the credit of
the disciples concerned, we may ask why it was not also
omitted from the first Gospel. Further, although St.
Luke does not record this special incident, he records
their φιλονεικία in xxii. 24.

39. ὃ πίνω πίεσθε. The difference in the use of tenses (see
Comm.) increases the vividness of the incident in trito-
Mark, when we compare the words used in Matthew.
Otherwise the language of the two accounts reveals a
close correspondence.

45. λύτρον. This word, ἅπ. λεγ. in the New Testament,
appears also in deutero-Mark. See Commentaries, and
p. 123 *supra*.

46-52. In the first Gospel we have two men cured when
Christ was leaving Jericho. In the third Gospel there
is only one man cured when Christ was entering it. In
the second only one man is mentioned; his name is given
and he was cured when Christ was leaving the city. Dr.
Wright (*Synopsis in loco*) claims that 'under the oral
hypothesis with its proto-Mark the whole mystery is
clear.' We agree with Dr. Wright that if St. Luke had
canonical Mark before him it is difficult to account for

the discrepancy, but against Dr. Wright we would urge
that a stereotyped tradition, sufficiently fixed to account
for the repetition of the unusual word λύτρον in v. 45,
would not have allowed discrepancy here. The theory
of three editions in documentary form affords a better
solution. There were probably two blind men, the
better known of which is referred to by name in the
Roman edition. See p. 126.

Chap. xi. 1-11. *Jesus enters Jerusalem in triumph.*
　　　　　　12-26. *The unfruitful fig tree. The cleansing of the
　　　　　　　　　　Temple.*
　　　　　　27-33. *The authority of Jesus.*

xi. 1. Βηθανίαν. In deutero-Mark we read Βηθφαγή and in
　　　Luke we have Βηθφαγὴ καὶ Βηθανίαν. There is
　　　uncertainty as to the text, but the longer reading in
　　　Mark seems to have been introduced to harmonise with
　　　Luke. See Wright *in loco.*
　　2. πῶλον. In deutero-Mark we have ὄνον καὶ πῶλον. This
　　　is probably an editorial alteration made to harmonise
　　　with the quotation from Zecharia.
　　4. The additional details in trito-Mark is characteristic of
　　　this edition.
　10. ὡσαννά. See Wright and Swete *in loco.*
　12-26. In deutero-Mark the cleansing of the Temple pre-
　　　cedes the cursing of the fig-tree. This does not suggest
　　　either a fixed oral tradition, or the use of canonical
　　　Mark by the editor of Matthew. It does, however,
　　　suggest a story told more than once, and a casual change
　　　in the order of events. The story of the fig-tree does
　　　not appear in the third Gospel. Now whether the
　　　interpretation of this incident be on the line of 'the
　　　power of faith,' or on that of 'the doom of an unfruitful
　　　nation' (see Romans xi. 17-22), the subject would
　　　have been appropriate to St. Luke with his Pauline
　　　point of view. It would thus be hard to account for
　　　his omission of it. We conclude that it did not appear
　　　in proto-Mark.
　27-33. The correspondence between all three accounts is
　　　here very close.

Chap. xii. 1-12. *National failure.   Parables.*
                13-40. *Discussion with Pharisees, Sadducees, and
                       others.*
                41-44. *The widow's mite.*

xii. 1-12. In proto-Mark and in trito-Mark only one parable is
           given, that of the Wicked Husbandmen.   In deutero-
           Mark we have also the parables of the Two Sons and of
           the Royal Marriage Feast.   These would appropriately
           find a place in an edition intended for Jewish Christians
           to whom the causes of national rejection needed to be
           made plain.   It is not necessary to refer these two
           parables to Q, merely because they do not appear in
           canonical Mark.   Even where all three give the same
           parable, the Jewish 'tendency' appears again in
           Matt. xxi. 43-45.

    4. ἐκεφαλίωσαν.   For this ἅπαξ λεγόμενον, see Wright and
       Swete *in loco.*

    9. In proto-Mark we have the addition ἀκούσαντες εἶπαν μὴ
       γένοιτο; the latter part of this sentence is, with the
       exception of this passage, only found in Paul.   It may
       therefore be an editorial addition inserted to give an
       adequate connection to the passage.

    11. After this verse in deutero-Mark we have an addition
        in xxi. 43, which again is appropriate to that edition
        as referring to the divine rejection of Israel.   Matt. xxi.
        44 is a harmonist's interpolation.

    14. κῆνσον.   See Comm. for the transliterated Latin word.
        St. Luke's φόρον is editorial.

    28-34. This incident is omitted in proto-Mark.   It is
        difficult to see why St. Luke should have omitted it if
        it was in the document before him.   Note that the
        rebuke of the Pharisees and Sadducees is again more
        severe in deutero-Mark.

    41-44. The story of the widow's mite does not appear in
        deutero-Mark.   Dr. Wright speculates that this
        'deliberate omission' may have been due to some local
        reason arising from the circumstances of the church in
        Alexandria.   To us it seems better to suppose that
        St. Mark inadvertently omitted it in preparing his
        second edition than that the editor suppressed it for local

reasons. St. Mark wrote 'as he remembered,' and the incident might escape recollection on one occasion, and be recalled on others.

xii. 42. λεπτὰ δύο ὅ ἐστι κοδράντης. In trito-Mark the value of the λεπτά is given in Roman coinage, the quadrans being one-fourth of an 'as.' See p. 128.

Chap. xiii. 1-37. *Eschatological discourses.*

xiii. 1 κατέναντι τοῦ ἱεροῦ. Another detail peculiar to trito-Mark. The difficult question of the 'Little Apocalypse' has been discussed above. See p. 111. The reader is also referred to Dr. Stanton's discussion of the question (*Gospels as Historical Documents*, pp. 115 ff.).

14. βδέλυγμα τῆς ἐρημώσεως. This expression is peculiar to the deutero-Mark. See Swete and Wright *in loco.* ἐν τόπῳ ἁγίῳ an addition to deutero-Mark which would be understood by Jewish Christians. The verses Luke xxi. 20 and 24, peculiar to that Gospel, are best explained as late additions made *ex post eventu.* See Wright and Commentaries.

Chap. xiv. 1-11. *The conspiracy against Jesus. His anointing at Bethany.*

12-25. *The Paschal Supper.*

26-42. *Jesus withdraws to the Mount of Olives. His agony.*

43-72. *The betrayal and the trial of Jesus.*

xiv. 3-11. The anointing of Jesus at Bethany has no place in the third Gospel; for the attempted identification of the ἁμαρτωλός in Luke vii. 37 with Mary of Bethany is now abandoned by practically all. Of this incident also we claim that it is inconceivable that St. Luke should suppress it as he must have done if canonical Mark was before him. Its non-appearance in proto-Mark is to be accounted for as above, p. 126.

12-25. On the Markan date for the Paschal Feast, see Wright and Swete.

17. St. Luke here inserts four verses which he derived from his special source (xxii. 15-18). See p. 181.

22. The giving of the cup before the bread is peculiar to St. Luke, who may have been influenced by the Pauline

order, 1 Cor. x. 15. St. Luke also makes the declaration
of betrayal come after the partaking of the bread and
wine. These facts, added to the considerable linguistic
difference from the Markan record, indicate that
St. Luke is in this section dependent largely upon his
special source. See p. 181.

xiv. 27-31. The prediction of St. Peter's unfaithfulness is given
in all three Gospels. No attempt is made by the editors
of the first and third Gospels to shield him. Yet this
supposed 'tendency' is held by many to account for
many of the differences between canonical Mark and
the other two Gospels. The Passion of our Lord and His
shrinking from 'the cup' is also given by all three
evangelists. See p. 121.

51-2. These verses, peculiar to the second Gospel, are
generally considered to have been added to the Petrine
Memoirs by St. Mark, and it is not improbable that the
evangelist himself was the νεανίσκος.

55. The failure to find witnesses against Jesus is not
recorded by St. Luke, and the identification of Peter by
the servants differs from that given in Matt. and Mark.
For example, in Mark xiv. 69 we read ἡ παιδίσκη πάλιν
where St. Luke writes ἕτερος. Such differences indicate
again St. Luke's special source. In the verse just cited
Matthew has ἄλλη, and we may well ask why the editor
should have altered canonical Mark if it was before him.
Such discrepancies constitute a common human feature
when a story is told more than once.

65. προφήτευσον. Deutero-Mark adds τίς ἐστιν ὁ παίσας σε;

72. ἐπιβαλών—a difficult word peculiar to trito-Mark. See
Field (*Notes on Translation, etc.*, p. 41), Wright and
Swete.

Chap. xv. 1-15. *Jesus before Pilate.*
16-41. *The Crucifixion.*
42-47. *The Burial of Jesus.*

Chap. xvi. 1-8. *The Resurrection.*

xv. The suicide of Judas is given in the first Gospel alone. Cf.
Acts i. 18. The reference in Acts i. shows this to have
been part of the Markan tradition in spite of its non-

appearance in canonical Mark—that is, if we may hold
that St. Luke derived the earlier chapters of Acts from
St. Mark. If the account of this incident be not referred
to deutero-Mark it is exceedingly difficult to account
for its appearance in the first Gospel.

xv. 1. In proto- and trito-Mark Pilate's name is given without
addition. In deutero-Mark he is called ὁ ἡγεμών. This
word is used to describe Pilate seven times in the first
Gospel, once in the third, and not at all in the second.
Pilate's title and position would be well known in both
Caesarea and Rome. For Herod's part in the trial of our
Lord, see *Oxford Studies in the Synoptic Problem*, p. 230,
and in this work p. 163.

7. μετὰ τῶν στασιαστῶν . . . ἐν τῇ στάσει; this is peculiar
to trito-Mark ; the fact of the insurrection and the names
of the insurgents would be known in Rome.

10. In deutero-Mark we have here the additional incident of
Pilate's wife's dream, and a little lower that of Pilate
washing his hands. Dr. Willoughby Allen refers these
to ' Palestinian tradition.' Their relation to what
precedes and to what follows certainly suggests interpolation into Markan matter.

16-41. The Lukan differences here—all derived from
St. Luke's special source—are to be carefully noted.

21. τὸν πατέρα Ἀλεξάνδρου καὶ Ῥούφου. Cf. Romans xvi.
13, and above, p. 126.

22. The variants in this verse are instructive :
Proto-Mark reads κρανίον (Latin Calvarium).
Deutero-Mark reads Γολγοθὰ ὅ ἐστι κρανίου τόπος
λεγόμενος.
Trito-Mark reads Γολγοθὰ ὅ ἐστι μεθερμηνευόμενον.

40. γυναῖκες. The first and third evangelists identify them
with the women that had followed Jesus from Galilee
and had ministered to Him. See p. 163.

xvi. 1-8. The different indications of time in the three editions
are :

Proto-Mark—ὄρθρου βαθέως.
Deutero-Mark—ὀψὲ σὲ σαββάτων τῇ ἐπιφωσκούσῃ εἰς
μίαν σαββάτων.
Trito-Mark—λίαν πρωῒ τῇ μιᾷ τῶν σαββάτων.

Note that the fourth evangelist seems to correct the Synoptic tradition, according to his custom, by writing πρωῒ σκοτίας ἔτι οὔσης. For the evidence for and against the theory of the mutilation of this chapter in Greek texts see the Commentaries.

ADDITIONAL NOTE II

SAYINGS FOUND IN MARKAN NARRATIVE

In the *Oxford Studies in the Synoptic Problem* (p. 267 ff.), Dr. Willoughby Allen, discussing the Book of Sayings and the first Gospel, describes certain sayings as being inserted by the editor of the first Gospel in Markan narrative. Such passages are as follows :

Matt.		Luke	
viii.	11-12.	xiii.	28-29.
ix.	13.		
xii.	5-7.		
	11-12.	xiii.	15 and xiv. 5.
xiii.	16-17.	x.	23-24.
xv.	13-14.	vi.	39.
xvi.	17-19.		
xviii.	7.	xvii.	1.
xix.	11-12.		
	28.		

Such a statement seems to be based upon the presupposition that the sayings of Jesus have no place in the Markan record. To us it seems far more likely that such sayings are not insertions made by the editor into Markan record, but that they belonged to that record, and are not to be regarded as taken from any book or collection of sayings by the editor of the first Gospel.

CHAPTER VI

THE LUKAN SOURCES

THE third Gospel presents us with a variety of special features each of which is of great importance with reference not only to the Gospel itself, but also to the conditions in which all three were prepared. The common authorship of this Gospel and the book of the Acts of the Apostles—an authorship which is now established as that of St. Luke, 'the beloved physician,' and the companion of St. Paul—enables us to bring together facts and features of both writings which throw considerable light upon each. Each is prefaced by a short introduction of great importance, and from this we learn :

1. That the Gospel was a ' treatise concerning all that Jesus began both to do and to teach until the day in which He was received up.' The words used, while they do not exclude the addition of other matter, seem to indicate that the more considerable parts of this Gospel consisted of a narrative portion which we have already seen was Markan in origin, and some collection of sayings or teachings of our Lord, which may possibly have been the collection made by St. Matthew, but which we have seen to be more probably drawn from some collection or collections of disjointed ' Logia ' used by both St. Matthew and St. Luke.

2. That, when St. Luke wrote, many accounts of the deeds and words of Jesus were in existence, and that these were in documentary form. The date

assigned to the production of the Gospel varies
with the scholar who discusses it. Some place it
as late as A.D. 95, others give the date as A.D. 70.
Those who assign the later date are largely influenced by the theory that St. Luke wrote his
book of the Acts with the writings of Josephus
before him. This, however, is far from receiving
a general acceptance. St. Luke's use of Markan
narrative need not determine the date to be even
so late as A.D. 70. For, as we have seen, the
probability is that he used a much earlier recension
of St. Mark's Gospel. It has, however, been held
that St. Luke differs so much from St. Mark in
his description of the doom of Jerusalem, and
where he differs seems so clearly to have been
influenced by what had actually transpired, that
few are willing to assign an earlier date than A.D.70.
The references in the introduction do not really
help us in deciding for a date later than A.D. 70 ;
for, if our inferences as to the nature of Q and as
to an earlier edition of St. Mark's writings hold
good, St. Luke might speak of ' many ' writings
at a much earlier date. The passages in which
he describes details of the destruction of Jerusalem,
and departs from Mark in doing so, are also open
to question. Those passages are xix. 43, 44,
xxi. 20 and 24. But, as Principal Bebb has shown,[1]
these need not indicate prophecy *ex post eventu.*
The question is not of vital importance from the
point of view of our present inquiry, and, while
we hold that possibly the date of this Gospel may
finally be fixed even earlier than A.D. 70, we shall
accept the date assigned by Harnack, who places
it between the years 78 and 93, inclining to the
earlier rather than the later of the two. That

[1] Hastings, *Bible Dictionary*, iii. p. 163.

these accounts were in documentary form appears
from the contrast between the words ἀνατάξασθαι
διήγησιν and παρέδοσαν.   For while the word
διήγησις might be used for a spoken narrative,
yet it is clear that St. Luke means to distinguish
between a tradition which has been ' delivered '
direct to him, and by which he has been able to
verify other accounts, and those accounts of which
he says that there are many.   The word ἀνατάξασθαι
too seems more appropriate to the formality of a
document than to the more uncertain oral tradition.
That this verification at first hand by those who
were ' eye-witnesses and ministers of the word '
was open to St. Luke is of immense importance,
as indicating an early date for his work and a
sufficient authority for the account which he gives.
We shall see, when we examine his sources, that the
phrase can be amply justified.

3. In compiling his Gospel from such sources, St. Luke
adopted an order which may fairly be styled
chronological.   For while the word καθεξῆς, which
is rendered in English versions ' in order,' need not
refer to order in time, yet a study of the writing
which follows, and a recognition of the difference
between his method of arranging the Logia of Jesus
and that followed by St. Matthew, shows that the
word was used in this sense.   Dr. Bartlet[1] considers
that the historical order is better preserved at the
beginning of the Gospel, and that ' it soon fades
away to be followed by a series of sections more
or less loosely linked together.'   He considers that
these links belong for the most part to the ' special
source ' used by St. Luke, who follows, in the earlier
part of his writing, the material which came to him
from St. Mark.   It is probable that this closer

[1] *Studies in the Synoptic Problem*, p. 345.

chronological ' nexus ' is due to the character of
the two writings before him, and to his respect for
each, rather than to any slackening of purpose to
maintain a chronological order on the part of St.
Luke. ' The Travel Document ' especially seems
to have been compiled as a series of notes taken
during a memorable journey, and the evangelist
would probably consider that the fact of the
journey gave an historical unity to the whole
document, and that it was unnecessary for him
to rearrange the incidents there mentioned. St.
Luke's respect for his sources seems to have been
so great, that even where we should have expected
an editor to have corrected his source in using it,
he does not do so. When he comes, however, to
the collection of ' sayings ' which he used, inasmuch as there was in these no attempt at chronological connection, he allows himself considerably
more freedom in arrangement.

The first of the sources used by this evangelist is that
which he obviously derived from St. Mark. The section
which deals with the birth and infancy of our Lord, which
is unique, will receive separate treatment, and as it is
obviously non-Markan it need not be considered here.
But omitting this for the present we notice in the Markan
section which follows several important differences from
canonical Mark. In iii. 1 he inserts a distinct chronological note, mentioning a Roman emperor by name and
thus fixing the point of time at which his narrative begins.
This is not found in Mark, and must be considered a distinctly Lukan addition intended to carry out his intention
of chronological treatment.[1] This is followed by an account
of the ministry of the Baptist, which is given in fuller
detail than we find even in the first Gospel, while it is so

[1] See Stanton, *op. cit.*, p. 228 ff.

much fuller than what we have in the second Gospel that in comparison the latter seems to be a mere reference introducing the more important ministry of our Lord. Now this account, taken with the baptism and temptation of our Lord, forms so conspicuous a feature of this Gospel that we are bound to consider its source. It cannot have come from canonical Mark. If it was so derived there is an amount of amplification suggested which we do not find in the rest of St. Luke's writing, for he keeps, as we have seen, very closely to his source. Nor can we assign it to ' oral tradition,' for its correspondence with the parallel section in the first Gospel suggests a written source, while the points of difference with that section show us that it was a similar, but not an identical, document which was before St. Luke. The commonly accepted explanation is that it was taken from Q, but, as we have seen, that takes for granted that Q contained a certain amount of narrative, and if this be allowed at the beginning of that document we may properly ask why it should not be allowed also at its close. But if Q contained a history of the Passion it must be considered to have been another Gospel, and the difficulties which gather round the theory of an Ur-Markus would be presented here again.[1] The difficulties which gather around Q are immensely reduced, if we can believe that this document was made up of discourses properly so called. Such difficulties would have to be faced if we were shut up to the conclusion that this section was taken from Q, but there is no need for us to accept that position. If the theory of a proto-Mark be allowed, and if this edition was that which came before the notice of St. Luke, we can see at once why his account of the Baptist's ministry was so much fuller than that which appears in the second Gospel, and we can see also why it should have so much in common with that given in the first Gospel, and yet differ from it in details. It

[1] See p. 108.

becomes unnecessary, too, to disturb the homogeneity of
Q, and that is a considerable gain.

Does the history of St. Luke then afford any occasion
in which he could have met with an early Markan version
of St. Peter's preaching ?   Now it is scarcely possible to
consider the Markan source of this Gospel without at
least some reference to the companion work which we
have in the Acts of the Apostles.   The masterly treatise
of Harnack, entitled *Luke the Physician*, has placed the
common authorship of the two books beyond dispute,
and in the book of the Acts we have a very distinct connection indicated between St. Mark and St. Luke.   In
the story of St. Peter's escape from prison we have an
intimate knowledge of the writer's acquaintance with
Mark's home ; he even knows the name of the servant maid
who opened the door to St. Peter.   He has recorded the
circumstances which led to the separation of St. Paul
from St. Mark in chapter xv.   It is probable that the
earlier portion of the Acts, which shows the prominence
of St. Peter in the earliest days of the Christian Church,
was derived from this 'Interpreter' of St. Peter's, and it
has been pointed out that the Greek of this section,
when compared with that of the 'We sections,' is more
Hellenistic and conforms to that of the Markan narrative
in the Gospels.

But if the first section of the Acts of the Apostles is
Markan, the second may be as clearly connected with
Philip.   Harnack points out the significance of the reference to Philip's removal to Caesarea in chapter viii., and
explains the abruptness with which the reference closes
by supplying the words ' and there I met him at a later
time.'   This later occasion of course is that recorded in
chapter xxi., where we are told that St. Paul and St. Luke
entered into the house of Philip the evangelist, one of the
seven deacons whose appointment to office is described
in chapter vi.   It is also mentioned that Philip had four

daughters ' who did prophesy.' With this may be compared the statement of Papias that these daughters of
Philip ' transmitted stories of the old days.' Harnack
argues from this that a possible source for the section of
the Gospel other than that of St. Mark and that derived
from Q, is to be found in that which came to the evangelist
through these daughters of Philip. At present, however,
we need only consider that here we have a distinct
association in Caesarea with certain Gospel stories. In
the Clementine Homilies and Recognitions there is also
an account of a disputation between St. Peter and Simon
Magus, and in the course of this description it is said that
one of the Christian converts of Caesarea sent to his friend
a work written at St. Peter's dictation, which had for its
theme the life of Christ. During the two years of St. Paul's
imprisonment St. Luke remained in Caesarea, and we
may be sure that he was not idle during those years. Yet
another link in our chain of evidence may be found in
connection with St. Peter's visit to Cornelius. On that
occasion the apostle would be accompanied by his
interpreter, and we have the statement of Clement of
Alexandria that St. Mark was asked by those who heard
St. Peter preach to write down what he had said, and that
St. Mark did this, and gave the writing to those who had
made the request. St. Clement says that this took place
in Rome, but this may have been due to some confusion in
Clement's mind between this Caesarean edition and the
later edition put forth by St. Mark at Rome. Some
uncertainty of this kind is indicated when Clement goes
on to say that St. Peter neither hindered nor encouraged
St. Mark in this work, whereas Origen states that St.
Mark was guided by St. Peter. It has often been pointed
out that St. Peter's address in the house of Cornelius is
practically an epitome of St. Mark's Gospel as we have it,
and we have only to consider that this document was
left by St. Mark at Caesarea to account for St. Luke's

coming into possession of an edition of St. Mark's Gospel which bears evidence of having had a Palestinian origin, and of having been written earlier than that which now bears the name of St. Mark in our canon. The references which connect Caesarea with some sort of Gospel history now become on this supposition intelligible, and though each by itself is not sufficient for us to draw any conclusion yet their cumulative force is considerable. This would make the date for the Markan source in the third Gospel as early as A.D. 42, in which year St. Mark went to Egypt.[1]

We need not discuss here St. Luke's treatment of the Markan narrative which he used. Students will find the question admirably dealt with both in Dr. Stanton's volume entitled *The Gospels as Historical Documents*, vol. ii. pp. 278 ff., and in Sir John Hawkins's *Horae Synopticae*, pp. 140 ff. The verbal alterations are such as might be expected from an editor whose Greek was less Hellenistic than that of St. Mark, and the frequent variations when recording works of healing indicate the medical interest and more scientific exactness of ' the beloved Physician.' This latter feature is fully worked out in Hobart's *The Medical Language of St. Luke*, and this again is criticised and amplified by Harnack in his work already quoted.[2] The insertion of additional matter and the non-appearance of incidents which are found in canonical Mark have already been dealt with in dealing with the Markan narrative (chap. vi.). Even in the linguistic differences as between this Gospel and that of St. Mark, it may well be that what appear to us to be alterations in word or phrase may have been due to variations between the Markan edition which St. Luke used and that which is familiar to us in the second Gospel. In referring to the difference between chapters i.-xii. and chapters xiii.-xxviii. in the book of the Acts, Sir John Hawkins points out that the divergence of the language from that of the

---

[1] See chap. v. p. 114. [2] *Luke the Physician*, pp. 175 ff.

Gospel is greater in the second than in the first part of
Acts, and this would show that St. Luke, dealing as he did
with a document, probably Markan, in the earlier section
and writing as himself an independent witness in the
second shows considerable respect to the document before
him. He would, we are assured, show the same respect to
the document which he used in drawing up his Gospel.
At the same time that his better style should appear in
modifications of St. Mark's language, and in the introduction of phraseology which he owed to his association
with St. Paul, need not occasion surprise to the student.
They certainly do not create any difficulty. They are
human features which are natural in a work prepared
under such conditions as St. Luke has outlined for us in
his introduction to the third Gospel. His abandonment of
the Markan source for another in his account of the post-
Resurrection appearances of our Lord will be dealt with
in another section, and it is necessary here only to record
the fact.

We have seen that St. Luke follows closely the Markan
narrative which he used, and that his respect for his source
is so great that he even includes words and phrases which
in his use of editorial privilege we should have expected
him to omit or to alter. This makes it all the more strange
that certain Markan sections are wanting from the third
Gospel, and many explanations of this have been offered.
Such omissions are to be found in the call of the first
disciples (Mark i. 16-20), the charge that Christ worked
miracles through collusion with Beelzebub (Mark iii. 19-30),
the fate of John the Baptist (Mark vi. 17-29), ' the great
omission' (Mark vi. 45, viii. 26), the treatment of offences
(Mark ix. 41-50), the condemnation of the fig-tree (Mark
xi. 11-14 and 19-25), and the anointing at Bethany (Mark
xiv. 3-9). This list of passages is not complete, but the
remainder is comparatively insignificant, and the passages
given may be considered typical.

The explanations usually given are as follows :

1. That they were accidentally omitted. Sir John Hawkins points out that St. Luke may have been misled into omitting 'the great omission' by passing from the mention of feeding multitudes in vi. 42 to that in Mark viii. 19-21 or from the name Bethsaida in vi. 45, to the same name in viii. 22.

2. That they were deliberately omitted because the evangelist knew that he had similar incidents or teaching in his Logian or some other source which he deliberately preferred. Dr. Stanton suggests this as explaining such omissions as that of the first call of disciples, the Beelzebub controversy, the subject of offences, and others.

3. That in the case of 'the great omission' St. Luke omitted the passage because he considered it unsuitable for his Gospel. Sir John Hawkins lays especial emphasis upon this in connection with the story of the Syrophenician woman.

4. That they were omitted by St. Luke in order to curtail his Gospel which seemed likely to be of inordinate bulk. Dr. Sanday inclines to this view.

To differ from authorities who have so fully established their position in the world of New Testament scholarship is fraught with peril, and I do so with the utmost diffidence. If there were no other solution in sight, one or other of these might afford relief to those who would account for the characteristics of these Gospels. But are we really shut up to these ? Dr. Sanday believes that features in canonical Mark are to be accounted for on the ground of a later recension of the text, but what if there were a recension not of the text alone, but of the whole Gospel, including subject matter as well as text, and made by St. Mark himself ? Would it not be possible to account for these

features of the third Gospel as being due to the fact that
they did not occur in the earlier edition of the Markan
narrative which St. Luke used ?   Let us take ' the great
omission ' more in detail.

It contains what one might consider to be matter
peculiarly attractive to St. Luke.   He reveals a distinct
sympathy with women which runs throughout the whole
of his Gospel, and as the follower of St. Paul he must have
been familiar with the attitude of that Apostle towards
the Gentiles, of whom St. Luke himself was one, and towards
the whole question of the Mosaic statutes and their relation
to the new life of the Spirit in Jesus Christ.   In this passage
he would find a story in which a woman and a Gentile was
received by Christ, and allowed a share in those blessings
which a narrow Pharisaism would reserve for the children
of Abraham.   That Christ even for the purpose of
strengthening the woman's faith treated her with contempt
by His use of the word ' dog ' we do not believe.   There
are other methods of creating or strengthening faith, and
this particular method seems far removed from that
which was Christ's.   Rather we believe that our Lord,
sick at heart with the bigotry, the spiritual pride, and the
gross materialistic interpretation of the law made by
Pharisees, seized the opportunity offered by the approach
of this woman to show to His disciples what Pharisaic
teaching was like when reduced to the concrete.   Here
stood a woman with the common human need of a mother's
anxiety for her daughter.   Must He treat her as one of
the unclean ?   To the Jew she was but one more ' dog of a
Gentile.'   But the woman was quick to see the indignant
irony that went with His words.   She accepted the current
phrase, unworthy as it was, and yet claimed that even
such a ' dog ' had a share at the banquet of heavenly grace.
Our Lord commended her faith and honoured it by the
gift which she sought.   That St. Luke of all evangelists
should choose this passage for omission is to us unthink-

able. The point of the whole story was that in spite of the
contempt felt by the Pharisees, and by Jews generally, a
contempt well known already to Gentiles and therefore
less likely to offend them in this setting, Christ agreed
with the woman that the blessings of the Covenant were
for the Gentiles also. It would be strange that St. Luke
should choose this passage so peculiarly ' Pauline ' for
omission.

It is possible to deal with each one of these so-called
' omissions ' in the same way. Dr. Stanton in discussing
the anointing at Bethany, again omitted by St. Luke,
points out that a better explanation is that in this case
' a reviser has inserted in the Markan Gospel a beautiful
and touching story connected with the events of Christ's life,
for which he wanted to find a place.' With this we would
agree, but make the further point that the ' reviser ' was
St. Mark himself. And if we are asked why it was suppressed by St. Mark in his earlier edition, we would answer
that the family at Bethany seems to have been in danger
of death, because Lazarus in himself was a complete
argument against the doctrine of the Sadducees, and the
story may have been suppressed for that reason. But
in a late edition published in Rome the difficulty was not
felt, and the story takes its place as one of perfect beauty
in the record of the Saviour's life.

The contention of the present work is one which brings
relief to all such questions. Sir John Hawkins seems to
feel this when, in writing on ' the great omission,' he says :
' It may have been unavoidable, because this whole division
of Mark may not yet have been inserted into that Gospel
when Luke used it. To use a now well-known expression,
it may have belonged to " a deutero-Mark." A good case
could be made for this account of the matter if we could
appeal to any appreciable linguistic difference between
this one-ninth part of our Mark and the remaining eight-
ninths. But we cannot do so. There is a general

uniformity of style and wording which is sufficient to show that—apart from small additions and modifications—it was composed by one author, or at least was thoroughly worked over by one editor.' [1]

This is an important concession by so great an authority on the whole question as the author of the *Horae Synopticae*. We would gladly accept it, and point out that if the case can be made out that the author of the deutero-Mark was St. Mark himself—that is, that in the first and second Gospels we have later and fuller editions of the Petrine Memoirs prepared by St. Mark—we secure at once the single authorship which leads to the uniformity of style and wording which Sir John Hawkins quite rightly finds in the record. The same explanation, we are convinced, will account for most if not all of the so-called ' Lukan omissions.'

The second of the sources used by St. Luke consisted of a collection of sayings. These are distributed by St. Luke over the whole field of his Gospel in accordance with his method, which, as we have seen, was to give a more or less chronological setting to his facts as recorded. The discussion of this source is complicated by the many uncertainties which gather around the whole question concerning the nature and contents of Q. In the third chapter of this work we have asked :

1. Whether this formula should be given to the Matthaean Logia as described by Papias, which many critics consider to be now hopelessly lost.
2. Whether we are to suppose that the term should be used for a work containing mostly ' sayings,' but also some admixture of narrative, and especially an account of the Passion.
3. Whether it should be given to a collection of Logia, thrown together without form or plan, containing

[1] *Oxford Studies*, p. 63.

genuine and spurious sayings of Christ, and with
no further connection between one saying and
another than the familiar introduction 'Jesus
said.'

4. We may also ask whether, supposing the formula Q
be used in any one of the above senses, St. Luke
used a 'Q' identical with that before St. Matthew,
or some other collection.

It will be sufficient to recapitulate here the conclusions
to which we came in chapter iii. We hold that the
Matthaean Logia described by Papias are not lost, but
exist in the first Gospel, thus accounting for the name
given to that Gospel from earliest times, though the work,
as a whole, is a compilation drawn up by some Jewish
Christian in Alexandria. We think that it would save
great confusion in discussion if the formula Q were not
used for a work consisting partly of sayings and partly
of narrative, thus making what would be to all intents and
purposes another 'Gospel,' of which no further trace
remains. We consider that the true source of the sayings
is to be found in those somewhat indiscriminate collections
of sayings, which seem to have existed in some number
in the early Church, and that the work of these inspired
evangelists consisted in the sifting of these sayings—a
work in which they were so marvellously guided that
they have preserved only those sayings which belong to
the one Divine Teacher who 'spake as never man spake.'

Last of all we have seen reason to suppose that while the
sayings that were used by St. Luke came before him in
documentary form, they belonged to a collection other
than that used by St. Matthew. All that we need add to
this part of our subject is to point out that in transcribing
these sayings St. Luke uses what seems to some a far
higher degree of verbal exactness than he does in dealing
with narrative (see Stanton, *op. cit.* p. 278). This, how-

ever, is better explained by supposing that in Markan narrative St. Luke records with a fidelity equal to that which he shows to his other sources the variations which belong to a writer giving to the Church an earlier edition of what he afterwards re-wrote in a slightly different form. In dealing with ' sayings ' he would have before him matter which was necessarily more fixed in expression.

The third Gospel contains three other sections in addition to those we have mentioned. These are the Nativity section embodied in chapters i. and ii., the section known by the name of ' the Travel Document ' consisting of the matter contained in ix. 51 - xviii. 14, and the post-Resurrection appearances of our Lord, xxiii. 54 - xxiv. 53. An attempt will be made in the present work to bring these three within the compass of a single source, but waiving that question for the present, and confining attention to the section commencing at chapter ix. 51, we notice its uniqueness both in contents and in style. It describes a portion of our Lord's ministry which is not dealt with by the other evangelists in anything approaching the same detail. It is the sole authority for such incomparable teaching as we derive from the Parables of the Good Samaritan, the Rich Man and Lazarus, the Importunate Widow, and the Prodigal Son. It is true that isolated sayings which appear in the other Gospels are found in these chapters, but that is not to be wondered at, when we recall the method in which these sayings were collected before St. Matthew made the topical arrangement of them which appears in the first Gospel. St. Mark, too, would incorporate in his narrative incidents which belong to this part of our Lord's ministry, such as that of Christ's reception of little children, or His treatment of the rich young ruler (Mark xiii. 13-51), but such sections in the second Gospel are out of their true chronological setting, and appear more like what we are convinced they were, incidents

recalled in the course of public preaching, and not parts of
a narrative given with strict chronological accuracy.   The
section contains several parables, a considerable proportion
of which are peculiar to St. Luke.,   Dr. Stanton considers
that these are to be accounted for as additions made to the
original Greek Logian document from which, as we have
seen, St. Luke drew a considerable part of his matter.
He concludes that these additions were Jewish-Christian
in origin, there being a distinct Hebraistic style discernible
throughout, and its birthplace seems to have been
Palestine.   He also holds that it came before the evangelist
in writing, but that certain passages gathered from oral
tradition were added by St. Luke himself, incidents in
the Passion and the post-Resurrection appearances of the
Lord being so accounted for.[1]

There is much in all this with which we cordially agree.
The documentary character of the source, its Jewish
features, and its Palestinian origin, seem to us to be fully
established by Dr. Stanton's scholarly analysis of details.
It does not seem to us, however, that the contents are
best accounted for by considering them to be additions
made to the Logian document supplemented by scraps
of oral tradition put into form by St. Luke.   Let us begin
with the parables.   These possess—as Dr. Stanton himself
points out—certain features as marked as they are interesting.   The parables that belong to the Logian document
deal with characteristics of the Kingdom of God.   Their
imagery was drawn largely from nature ; they illustrate
the coming of the Kingdom, its growth, and its final con-
summation.   Their interpretation was to some extent a
matter of difficulty ; the clue to that intrepretation had
to be given by the great Teacher before their meaning
became clear.   They are above all distinctly Christological,
and, until the centrality of Christ and His supremacy
within the Kingdom became clear, they were to the common

[1] *Op. cit.* pp. 239-40.

people enigmatic. But the miracles peculiar to St. Luke which occur in this section have nothing to do with the Kingdom. To quote from Dr. Stanton : ' They are concerned with human emotions and motives, inner debatings and actions, which are vividly described ; they are in fact short tales of human life. . . . Once more no subsequent, separate interpretation could be required, or asked for, in the case of these parables. They bear their moral on the face of them, and in several instances it is driven home by an emphatic saying at the conclusion.' [1] That parables should appear throughout the whole course of our Lord's teaching is nothing more than we should expect, and that having made clear to His immediate followers the principles of the Kingdom of God, as He had come to establish it, He should go on at some later period in His ministry to deal with those subtleties of the human heart which are universal in experience and need no interpreter, is exactly in keeping with the development of His teaching. This characteristic of the parables which appear in this section creates a unity which covers the whole section, and is accentuated by other features which belong to it, and which will appear when we have dealt with it as a whole.

The passage is introduced by the words ' And it came to pass when the days were well nigh fulfilled that He should be received up, He steadfastly set His face to go to Jerusalem.' Throughout the whole section Christ is described as journeying up to Jerusalem. In the former part of the Gospel the scene is entirely and consistently Galilean, but in this section Galilee is left behind. The route is first eastwards to Perea and then through that country to Jerusalem. For this reason scholars have agreed to give the section the name of ' the Travel Document,' while others prefer to describe it as ' the Perean Section.' Now this element of movement from one part

of the country to another makes a second unity for the
passage.   It may be described as ' notes taken on the
course of a memorable journey.'   Dr. Arthur Wright
does not allow any such unity as is here assigned to this
section. He considers it to be a collection of undated
material made up of ' fragments which came to St. Luke,
as he taught at Philippi, by every ship.'   This statement
accords with the requirements of an oral tradition as basis
for the Gospel, but it entirely fails to account for outstanding features of the section.   For in addition to
features already referred to we find a strong Samaritan
element in this portion of the third Gospel.   Nearly every
instance in which the Samaritans are mentioned by the
Synoptic writers occurs in this section, nor are they
mentioned without indications of strong sympathy.
This fact is considered so significant that some scholars
assign the section to St. Philip.   We know that St. Luke
spent two years in the house of that evangelist in Caesarea,
and we are told in the Acts of the Apostles that ' Philip
went down to the city of Samaria and preached unto
them the Christ' (Acts viii. 5).   It is extremely likely
that the chapters which describe the ministry of Philip
in the Acts of the Apostles are due to the intercourse
between these two men in Caesarea.   The conjecture that
the section in the Gospel is also to be attributed to that
source is attractive, but considering that the events described are not limited to Samaria, and bearing in mind
the repeated emphasis laid upon the fact of the journey
(see ix. 56, x. 1-38, xiii. 22, xvii. 11, xviii. 35, xix. 11-29),
it seems to us more probable that while the incidents
recorded were collected by one who from sympathy with
Samaritans would treasure up any reference to them made
by our Lord, that one belonged to the little band of men
and women who accompanied Him upon the memorable
journey.   To them the incidents of that journey were
likely to have been indelibly fixed upon the memory, and

very early, we may be sure, they were committed to the
safer keeping of some written record.

There is yet another feature of this section which indeed
appears in other parts of the third Gospel as well as in
the Acts of the Apostles, and this is the intimate knowledge
shown of incidents connected with the court of Herod
(see Luke iii. 1, 19, viii. 3, ix. 7-9, xiii. 31, xxiii. 7-12 ;
Acts xii.). In the Acts St. Luke seems to set the authority
of his source against that of Josephus from whose narrative
of Herod's death he differs considerably. Last of all there
is the strongly marked sympathy with women which runs
throughout the Gospel. So frequent are the indications
of a woman's interest that the Gospel is sometimes called
' The Woman's Gospel.' It is most marked in the section
which deals with the Nativity of our Lord, speaking of
which Sir William Ramsay says : ' There is a womanly
spirit in the whole narrative which seems inconsistent
with the transmission from man to man.' This feature
meets us again both in the closing section of the Gospel
and in this 'Travel Document.' Is it possible to bring these
three sections of the third Gospel within the compass of a
single source ? If we could do so the gain would be very
great, for it is generally accepted as a canon of criticism
that the multiplication of sources is to be avoided if
possible. Now in the opening verses of the eighth chapter
we are told that there accompanied cur Lord certain
women who ' ministered unto Him of their resources,'
and of these three names are mentioned,—Mary Magdalene,
Susanna, and Joanna, the wife of Chuza, Herod's steward.
At the close of the twenty-third chapter we are told that
their ministry continued after their Master had been
crucified, and that they proceeded to prepare the spices
which would be required for embalming His body. Of these
women we are told that they had come with Jesus out of
Galilee, and it is easy to infer that they would be likely to
treasure up the precious teaching of their Master whom

they served with such devotion. Of the three names that of Joanna attracts attention. Her name does not appear in the other Synoptic Gospels. St. Luke is the one evangelist who has rescued her name from oblivion. Only to him has she seemed to be of interest, as indeed she would be if through her devotion to Christ he had been put in possession of these priceless records. In the first chapter of the Acts her name does not appear, but we are told that the disciples continued in prayer ' with the women, and Mary the Mother of Jesus.' The reference can only be to some well-known band of women who were now joined by the Mother of our Lord, and there can be no reasonable doubt that they were those who had been the companions of Jesus during the latter part of His ministry. Harnack recognises the necessity of finding some womanly element among the authorities consulted by St. Luke, but thinks that this may be supplied by the daughters of Philip. These, however, do not seem to have been associated with our Lord during His ministry, nor do they supply what we need to account for the knowledge of Herod's court which belongs to this source. No better authority for this could be found than what is given us in the wife of his steward Chuza.

Dr. Bartlet contributes to the *Oxford Studies in the Synoptic Problem* a paper on the sources of St. Luke's Gospel in which he allows that the features of ' the great insertion ' which Dr. Stanton has discussed, and to which reference has already been made in this work, are fairly established, especially the Hebraistic style prominent in the Nativity section, but appearing also in ' the Travel Document,' and the Resurrection story. The agreement of these two authorities on the unity underlying these different sections goes far to support the claim of a common authorship for them all. Dr. Bartlet also agrees with Dr. Stanton in reducing the Lukan sources to two, ascribing these three sections together with the Logia to a source

which he calls ' S ' and which was unified in tradition with
Q. The difference between Dr. Stanton and Dr. Bartlet
is found in this, that the latter ' sees no evidence that Q
was ever written down before it was so in Luke's S.' Taking
Q to represent ' the original apostolic tradition ' he con-
ceives it to have come before St. Luke in the form of oral
tradition. Dr. Stanton, however, considers that it came
to him in documentary form. But whether this particular
source was oral or documentary—and it seems to us that
the latter is the more likely, as Dr. Stanton shows—it
is clear that the question of the nature and contents of
Q, perhaps the most vexed question of all that concern
the Synoptic Problem, must first be settled before we can
arrive at any general agreement as to the relation of this
section of the third Gospel to Q. Dr. Bartlet considers
that Q included the Passion story, a theory already discussed.[1] There is also something too formal about the
theory of ' an original apostolic tradition ' existing at the
time when this matter came before St. Luke. It contains
an element of Canonicity which belongs to the second
century rather than the first, and to us it seems probable
that the origins of the Gospel were very much more simple
than an apostolic tradition would indicate. The outstanding feature of the different parts of the Gospels is
individual rather than collective, and this is true whether
we consider the Markan narrative, the Matthaean sayings,
or ' the great insertion ' of St. Luke. The homogeneity
of this section is another argument against the idea that
all this matter came to St. Luke in the form of oral tradition.
Such a tradition would come along many lines, and be
likely to reveal many tendencies, whereas this section
reveals in the character of the parabolic teaching and of
the Samaritan interest an individual point of view which
does not go with an apostolic tradition in oral form. Nor
is it an answer that such a point of view would be conferred

[1] See p. 42.

by St. Luke the redactor. The Hebraistic feature of the
writing makes that the most unlikely solution of all.
To account for all the characteristics of this section we
need a Jewish Christian of Palestine, a companion of
Christ during His journey from Galilee to Jerusalem, one
who had to do with Samaritans and also had knowledge
from within of Herod's court. All these elements are
supplied by Joanna, the wife of Herod's steward, whose
name appears with such marked emphasis in this Gospel.

There remain for our consideration two sections of this
Gospel. The two chapters which make up what is called
' the Nativity Section ' and the chapter with which St.
Luke closes his record are unique in the Gospel story.
They belong neither to Markan narrative nor to Q nor any
other collection of sayings. We hold that there is good
reason for supposing that they reveal a common authorship.
For not only does St. Luke here depart from the Markan
narrative, but all three chapters belong to a Judaean
tradition rather than to a Galilean. To the author the
infancy of John the Baptist, and the circumstances attending his birth, were matters of great interest, and a necessary
introduction to the account of the birth of the Messiah.
The references to Anna and Simeon and to Christ's inter-
view with the doctors in the temple are parts of a tradition
which grew up around Jerusalem rather than around
some centre in Galilee. So in the last chapter Jerusalem
is spoken of as ' the city,' and the reference to the temple
in verse 53 is significant. The linguistic characteristics
of the one section appear also in the other ; both are
distinctly Hebraistic, and expressions are found in both
which are not found in other parts of the third Gospel.[1]
That there should have been a Judaean tradition as well
as that more distinctly Galilean tradition which St. Mark
has handed down to us will scarcely be denied by any one.
That a Church which originated and grew up in the Holy

[1] See additional notes, pp. 173 ff.

City should have remained content with a record wholly concerned with the ministry of our Lord in Galilee can scarcely be believed, and that St. Luke should turn to the record of that tradition to set forth the circumstances attending both the birth of Jesus and His Ascension is the most natural thing in the world. It is the recognition of his departure from the Markan narrative in recording the post-Resurrection appearances of Christ which offers the best solution of the difficulties which beset this part of the Gospel narrative. The Markan account is preserved for us in the first Gospel, for the mutilation of the last chapter in canonical Mark makes anything like a close comparison of the two impossible. That account follows the general plan of the Markan narrative. Its scene is entirely Galilean, but when we see that St. Luke prefers in this instance to give those appearances of the risen Lord which occurred in and about Jerusalem, we account at once for the differences which undoubtedly exist between the one account and the other.

Returning to the Nativity section, we notice that, whether St. Luke modified it in part or not, the original story has a source which is distinctly feminine. The story differs from that in the first Gospel exactly as Mary's story would differ from that of Joseph. The mother of our Lord would naturally refrain from speaking of that which was known only to her husband and herself. She ' hid all these things in her heart.' But after the resurrection she would as naturally feel that she was bound to impart that story to those who like herself would after that event know that the Jesus whose earthly life they had in large measure shared was indeed the very Messiah. Yet the modesty and reserve which had kept her silent in this matter would cause her to impart her great secret only to the women who were with her in the upper room while they waited for the coming of the promised Comforter. Among these, as we have seen, was Joanna,

and if the wife of Herod's steward may be supposed to
have been better educated than the majority of Jewish
women, she would be most likely to put on record what she
had received, and to add her own contribution to the
story. In his admirable work entitled *Luke the Physician*,
Harnack says : ' A Greek source cannot lie at the foundation of chapters i. and ii. of St. Luke's Gospel ; the correspondence between their style and that of Luke is too
great ; it would have been necessary that the source
should have been re-written sentence by sentence. It is
possible, but not probable, that for the narrative part an
Aramaic source was translated. The Magnificat and the
Benedictus at all events are St. Luke's composition.' It
is difficult to go so far as Harnack does in ascribing even
parts of this essentially Jewish composition to a Gentile
like St. Luke. The Lukan style is not admitted by Dr.
Stanton, whose paragraph on this point should be carefully
read. He says,[1] ' While then it may be allowed that the
third evangelist might himself have written the hymns in
Luke i. and ii., it does not appear that their style is un-
questionably distinctive of him. And in the character of
their Messianic expectation there is strong reason for
thinking that they cannot be his. It would have been
difficult even for a Jewish Christian, and wellnigh impossible for a Gentile, such as the author of the Lukan writings
probably was, and indeed must have been if he was Luke
the companion of St. Paul, to have placed himself at, and
adhered so consistently to, a point of view which preceded
the Passion and the Resurrection.' To the present writer
it seems even less likely than apparently it does to Dr.
Stanton that the hymns can have been written by St.
Luke. The whole section is without seam or division,
and the hymns in particular are the product of a mind
steeped in the imagery of Hebrew poetry. Least of all

[1] *Op. cit.* p. 225. For a three-document hypothesis see *Expos. Times*, xi.
473 and xx. 112.

do the chapters suggest fragments of oral tradition. One mind conceived the exquisite portrayal, and if that mind was that of a woman then it seems most likely that we must seek for her among those women who were associated with our Lord in the course of His ministry and afterwards with His mother.

In dealing with the common characteristics of the matter peculiar to St. Luke we have anticipated what should be said of the last section of this Gospel in which St. Luke gives his account of the post-Resurrection appearance of our Lord. Dr. Stanton holds that the accounts of incidents in the history of the Passion and appearance of the Risen Christ owe their written form to St. Luke, who gathered them probably from oral tradition. There is, however, nothing in the passage which would bear out this assumption, and against it we would place the Hebraistic style which appears in chapter xxiv. as it appears in the Nativity section. It is possible that there is but one source for the two sections, and the way in which Joanna's name is introduced is significant. It appears in xxiv. 10, and many critics point out that the verse reads somewhat like an interpolation. We hold that if so it was an interpolation made by the evangelist himself, and what could be more natural than that he should thus record the name of the woman to whom he owed this special contribution to the Gospel story.

To sum up this discussion of the Lukan sources we hold that they were three in number. The first consists of an account of Christ's ministry in Galilee derived from St. Mark, but not from the second Gospel as we have it in the Christian Canon. The narrative used by St. Luke for this part of his Gospel was earlier than that which appears either in the first or in the second Gospel. Its birthplace was Palestine, and if we must define still closer we would place it in Caesarea. We would account thus for the fuller reference in this Gospel to the ministry of the

Baptist and to the Baptism and Temptation of our Lord, while at the same time the theory offers a simple but sufficient explanation for the non-appearance of sections which are to be found in later and fuller editions of the Markan narrative. This does not preclude St. Luke's use of editorial privilege. He would modify the style where it seemed to him to be defective, and impress his own personality upon the record by employing medical terms where it seemed to him better to do so. He would also supply such chronological connections as seemed to be desirable to one who wished to set forth the sayings and doings of Jesus ' in order,' and he would distribute his material whether derived from this or from other sources so as to secure this object.

His second source was undoubtedly a collection of the sayings of our Lord. As coming from the same great Teacher these would bear a great amount of similarity to those which appear in the first Gospel, but there seems good reason to believe that the collection used by this evangelist differed considerably from those employed by St. Matthew when he made his notable compilation of the same Teacher's words. Whether the collection before St. Luke was earlier or later than that before St. Matthew it is useless to enquire. It may well be that ' forasmuch as many have taken in hand to draw up a narrative concerning those matters ' more than one collection was extant, and the two collections may well have existed side by side.

The third source we consider to have been a document containing at least the section on the Nativity, the account of Christ's journey from Galilee to Jerusalem with His teaching on the way, and details of the Passion and Resurrection. We hold that there is good reason drawn entirely from internal evidence that this was the work of Joanna.[1] Her relation through her husband both to

[1] I arrived at this conclusion by independent study, but it has been

Herod and to the Samaritans, her Jewish birth and education, and her association with the mother of our Lord, and her strong womanly sympathy all combine to make the introduction of her name by St. Luke significant.

EXCURSUS I

ANALYSIS OF THE THIRD GOSPEL

CHAP. i. 1-4. INTRODUCTION. EDITORIAL.

Chaps. i. ii. The birth and infancy of Jesus. Special source.

iii. 1-2. Editorial addition.

3-22. Ministry of John the Baptist. Baptism of Jesus. Markan source.

23-38. Genealogy of Jesus. Special source.

iv. 1-13. The temptation. Markan source.

14-30. The preaching of Jesus at Nazareth. Special source.

31-44. Works of healing. Markan source.

v. 1-39. Jesus calls His Disciples, cures a leper and a paralytic, and is entertained by Matthew. Markan source.

vi. 1-16. Controversy with the Pharisees on the question of the Sabbath. Jesus withdraws to a mountain. Markan source.

17-49. Jesus addresses His Disciples. Logian document.

vii. 1-10. Cure of the Centurion's servant. Markan source.

11-17. Jesus raises the son of the widow at Nain. Special source.

18-35. Testimony concerning the Baptist. Markan source.

29-30. Special source.

vii. 36-viii. 3. The woman that was a sinner at Simon the Pharisee's house. Special source.

pointed out to me by my friend, Dr. J. H. Moulton, that I have been anticipated by Dr. Sanday. See Hastings' *Dictionary of the Bible*, art. 'Jesus Christ,' p. 639. I can only say that I am delighted to find myself in agreement with so great a scholar.

viii. 4-21. Parables and Discourses.　Logian document.
22-56. Mighty works.　Markan source.

ix. 1-17. Mission of the Twelve, and death of the Baptist.
Markan source.

18-27. Confession of Peter; announcement of Passion.
Markan source.

28-45. The Transfiguration, and cure of demoniac boy.
Markan source.

46-50. Questions as to greatness, and toleration.
Markan source.

51-xviii. 14. The journey from Perea.　Special source.

xviii. 15-30. Little children, and the rich young ruler.
Markan source.

30-43. Announcement of Passion.　Healing of the blind.
Markan source.

xix. 1-27. Zacchæus, and the parable of the Pounds.
Special source.

28-48. Triumphal entry, and cleansing of the Temple.
Markan source.

xx. 1-47. Controversy with Pharisees and others.　Markan
source.

xxi. 1-4. The Widow's Mite.　Markan source.

5-38. Eschatological teaching.　Markan source.

xxii. 1-38. The plot against Jesus.　The Paschal Supper.
Markan source.

38-71. The agony of Jesus.　His betrayal.　Markan
source.

xxiii. 1-5. The trial of Jesus.　Markan source.

6-19. Jesus, Herod, and Pilate.　Special source.

20-26. Jesus delivered to be crucified.　Markan source.

27-31. The weeping daughters of Jerusalem.　Special
source.

32-56. The Crucifixion of Jesus.　Markan source.

xxiv. 1-53. The Resurrection of Jesus, His appearance to His
disciples, and Ascension into Heaven.　Special
source.

EXCURSUS II

THE 'SPECIAL SOURCE' OF THE THIRD GOSPEL: ANALYSIS WITH NOTES.

The special source is indicated in the following passages :—
Chaps. i. and ii.

     iv. 14-30.
     vii. 11-17, 29-30.
     vii. 36-viii. 3.
     ix. 51.-xviii. 14.
     xix. 1-27.
     xxiii. 6-19, 27-56.
     xxiv.

Chap. i. 1-4. Editorial Introduction. See p. 148.

          5-35. On the general question of Semitisms in Synoptic Gospels, see Dalman, *The Words of Jesus*, pp. 17 ff. 'Genuine Hebraisms' are almost exclusively peculiarities of St. Luke's Gospel.
1. The section begins with a reference to Herod. See p. 163. The use of the introductory ἐγένετο is characteristic of the source. It is sometimes used absolutely as here and also in i. 8, 23, 59 ; ii. 1, 6, 15, 46 ; vii. 11 ; viii. 1 ; ix. 18, 28, 37, 51. Often with ἐν τῷ followed by an Infinitive. The phrase is found in each of the five formulæ used by the editor of the first Gospel in passing from the Logia to the Markan source and in one other place. It is used four times in Mark, not at all in John, and forty-two times in Luke. See Plummer's *Comm. on this Gospel*, p. 45.

Chap. i. 5. ἐκ τῶν θυγατέρων Ἀαρών (cf. xiii. 16 and xix. 9).
        6. ἐναντίον τοῦ θεοῦ. This use, with that of ἐνώπιον, is common in the LXX. For its use in this source see i. 6, xxiv. 19. ἐνώπιον appears in v. 15 of this chapter and in twenty-three other passages

in this Gospel. In does not appear in Matthew or in Mark, and only once in John. (See Dalman, *op. cit.* p. 31.) Of the Lukan passages all but four are in sections taken from the special source. πορευόμενοι, common in LXX, Psalm cxix. 1. In this Gospel see ix. 53, xxiv. 13.

8. ἐν τῷ with Infinitive. Once in Matt. and Mark, not at all in John, but twenty-five times in Luke. See ix. 36, 51; xi. 1; xxiv. 4, 15. κ.τ.λ. See Dalman, *op. cit.* p. 33.

i. 19. εὐαγγελίζεσθαι. Used as in the Old Testament for announcing good tidings.

20. ἰδού. Hebraistic. The word appears fifty-five times in this Gospel. ἔσῃ σιωπῶν. For the use of εἶναι, with the participle, see Dalman, p. 35, and Moulton, *Prolegomena,* p. 226.

30. χάριν εὗρες is Hebraic (cf. ii. 40, 52, xvii. 7). The word χάρις does not appear in the first two Gospels. In the 'we' sections of Acts it is used in the Pauline sense.

39-56. *The meeting of Mary and Elizabeth.*

43. ἵνα. See p. 184, and Stanton, *Gospels as Historical Documents,* ii. p. 312.

50. εἰς γενεὰς καὶ γενεάς, cf. εἰς γενεὰν καὶ γενεάν, Psalm lxxxix. 2.

51. ἐποίησεν κράτος and ἐν βραχίονι are both Hebraisms. See Plummer *in loco.* ὑπερηφάνους διανοίᾳ. Frequent in LXX.

54. μνησθῆναι ἐλέους. Cf. Psalms xxv. 6 and xcviii. 3.

57-79. *Birth of John and song of Zecharias.*

58. ἐμεγάλυνεν ἔλεος (cf. Genesis xix. 19).

68. τῷ λαῷ (cf. vii. 16, xxiv. 19). ἐπεσκέψατο. 'Used in the Hebrew sense of Divine visitation by St. Luke alone.' See Plummer *in loco.*

69. κέρας σωτηρίας. A common Old Testament metaphor (cf. Psalm xviii. 3).

70. ἀπ᾽ αἰῶνος. Peculiar to St. Luke (cf. Acts iii. 21, xv. 18.

76. πρὸ προσώπου. A Hebraistic construction. Dalman, p. 29.

i. 78-79. The genitives of characterising quality are Hebraistic.

Chap. ii. 1-5. (Editorial Introduction.)

6-20. *The birth of Jesus.*

8. φυλάσσοντες φυλακάς. This Hebraistic form of expression occurs throughout this source (cf. Mark v. 9, and Luke vii. 29, xii. 50, xvii. 24, xxii. 15, and xxiii. 46). See Dalman, p. 34.

9. ἐπέστη. A Lukan word used of supernatural appearances (cf. ii. 38, and xxiii. 11).

10. τῷ λαῷ. So also in i. 68, and vii. 16.

11. ἐν πόλει Δαυείδ. Hebraistic.

15. ἴδωμεν τὸ ῥῆμα. Hebraistic.

19. συνβάλλουσα. Peculiar to St. Luke. See Plummer on i. 66.

21-40. The Circumcision of Jesus and His Presentation in the Temple.

22. αἱ ἡμέραι τοῦ καθαρισμοῦ. A Hebraism which appears again in iv. 16, xiii. 14, 16, xiv. 5, xxii. 7.

25. προσδεχόμενος. This verb occurs again in v. 38, and in xxiii. 51. See Dalman, p. 109.

26. ὁ Χριστὸς κυρίου. A similar phrase occurs no less than nine times in chapters i. and ii.

38. ἐν αὐτῇ τῇ ὥρᾳ. A Lukan expression which occurs in x. 21, xi. 12, xiii. 31, xx. 19, and xxiv. 33.

48. ὀδυνώμενοι. Three times in Luke but not elsewhere in the Gospels (cf. xvi. 24, 25).

49. ἡλικία for 'stature.' So again in xix. 3.

Chap. iv. 14-30. *The Discourse at Nazareth.*

16. ἐν τῇ ἡμέρᾳ τῶν σαββάτων. This phrase does not occur in the other Gospels. In the third Gospel it occurs here, and also in xiii. 14, 16, and xiv. 5.

20. ἦσαν ἀτενίζοντες (cf. i. 20, xiii. 10, xiv. 10, xv. 1).

21. ἤρξατο λέγειν. Hebraistic. See Dalman, p. 27, and cf. vii. 38, 49, xi. 29, 53, xii. 1, xv. 25, xxiii. 30.

27. ἐν τῷ Ἰσραήλ. A distinctly Jewish use (cf. i. 16, 54, 68, 80, ii. 25, 32, 34, vii. 9, xxii. 30, xxiv. 21).

Chap. vii. 11-17. *Jesus raises the son of the widow of Nain.*

It is to be noted that this section, peculiar to the third Gospel, contains in the space of half a dozen verses characteristics which distinctly connect it with chapters i. and ii. We assign it without hesitation to the same source.

11. ἐγένετο. See note on i. 5.

12. καὶ ἰδοὺ ἐξεκομίζετο. See note on i. 20.

13. ὁ κύριος. This title of Christ does not appear in the other Synoptic Gospels. In Luke it is used here, and also in x. 1, 39, xi. 39, xvii. 5, 6, xviii. 6, xxiv. 34 ; all passages are from the special source.

16. τὸν λαόν (cf. i. 68 and xxiv. 19).

17. 'Ιουδαία. Used in Matthew and Mark for the province of Judaea, but used here, and also in i. 5, vi. 17, xxiii. 5, xxiv. 19, for Palestine.

29-30. These two verses also seem to be taken from St. Luke's special source. The following expressions should be noted.

29. ὁ λαός. See 16 above and i. 68 and xxiv. 19, ἐδικαίωσαν (cf. Psalm lxxii. 13, Ezekiel xvi. 51, Jeremiah iii. 11, cf. x. 39, and xviii. 14. βαπτισθέντες τὸ βάπτισμα. See note on ii. 8, and cf. xxii. 15.

30. νομικοί. In Matthew and Mark the word generally used is γραμματεῖς, but νομικός appears here and also in x. 25, xi. 45, 46, 52, 53, xiv. 3.

36. κατεκλίθη. The middle voice is used here and in xiv. 8 and xxiv. 30, but nowhere else in the New Testament. Note that in the Markan passage, ix. 14, the active voice is used.

36-viii. 3. *Simon the Pharisee and the woman that was a sinner.* This section is peculiar to the third Gospel. Christ's vindication of the *woman's* action is to be noticed (see p. 163), and the section is followed by a reference to the women who followed our Lord from Galilee. Among the names that of Joanna appears for the first time. See pp. 163 ff.

36. κατακλίνεσθαι. See note on v. 36 of this chapter.

vii. 38. ἤρξατο βρέχειν. See note on iv. 21.

41. χρεοφειλέτης. This word appears only here and in xvi. 5 in the New Testament. The second passage as well as this belongs to the special source.

49. πορεύου εἰς εἰρήνην. 'A Hebrew formula of peace and goodwill with special fulness of meaning.' Dr. Stanton speaks of this section as being derived from oral tradition by St. Luke. But such linguistic peculiarities as it possesses show a connection with other portions of this Gospel, and it is better to assign it with them to St. Luke's special source.

Chap. ix. 51-56. *Inhospitable Samaritans.* St. Luke's 'great insertion' (see p. 161) begins at this point. Note the introductory words which indicate a journey and the Samaritan reference (see p. 162).

51. ἐγένετο. See note on i. 5.

51. πρόσωπον ἐστήρισεν. A Hebraism. Plummer compares Jeremiah xxi. 10, Ezekiel vi. 2, etc.

52. πρὸ προσώπου. A Hebraism, which occurs again in vii. 27 and x. 1. See Dalman, p. 29.

57-62. *Conditions of discipleship.* For the relation of this section to the parallel in Matthew, see Plummer.

61. ἀποτάξασθαι. See also xiv. 33. εὔθετος. Used again xiv. 35. Dalman, p. 119.

Chap. x. 1-16. *The Mission of the Seventy.*

6. υἱὸς εἰρήνης. A Hebraism to denote 'one closely identified with' (cf. 'The sons of the prophets' in the Old Testament, and such phrases as τέκνα σοφίας, vii. 35, and υἱὸς τῆς ἀπωλείας, John xvii. 12).

17-20. *The Return of the Seventy.*

21-24. *The Mysteries of the Kingdom.*

21. ἠγαλλιάσατο. The only other passage in which this word occurs in Luke is i. 47. The author uses χαίρω quite frequently. εὐδοκία ἐγένετο ἔμπροσθέν σου. A distinct Hebraism.

25-37. *The parable of the good Samaritan.*

25. νομικός. See note on vii. 40.

x. 29. δικαιοῦν ἑαυτόν. See note on vii. 35.

33. Σαμαρείτης. See p. 162.

37. ποιεῖν ἔλεος μετά (cf. i. 58).

38-42. *In the house of Martha and Mary.*

38. ἐγένετο ἐν τῷ with Infin. See note on i. 5.

39. τοῦ Κυρίου (cf. v. 17 and vii. 13.)

Chap. xi. 1-15. *Prayer, and the cure of the dumb demoniac.*

1. ἐγένετο ἐν τῷ εἶναι. Note on i. 5.

5. τίς ἐξ ὑμῶν ; This phrase appears in Luke, but only in this 'Travel Document' in which it is frequent. See xi. 11, xii. 25, xiv. 5, 28, 31, xv. 4, xvii. 7. In Matthew it appears two or three times, but always in Logian sections.

7. μὴ κόπους πάρεχε (cf. xviii. 5.)

14. ἐγένετο, followed by gen. abs. ' Any one desiring to collect instances in favour of a Hebrew primitive Gospel would have to name in the first rank this καὶ ἐγένετο.' Dalman, p. 32.

16-19. *Signs, and the blasphemy of the Pharisees.*

20. ἐν δακτύλῳ θεοῦ. ' Luke seems to be fond of Hebraistic anthropomorphisms, i. 51, 66, 73.' Plummer *in loco.*

27-28. *True relationship to Christ.* The incident brings again into prominence the 'womanly reference' characteristic of this source.

29-32. The sign of Jonah. This section as well as others in this chapter (notably vv. 24-26) appear in Matthew. They may have found their way into the collection of Logia used by St. Matthew independently of the source to which St. Luke was indebted.

33-36. *The inner Light.*

37-54. *Our Lord's denunciation of hypocrisy.*

39. γέμει ἁρπαγῆς. Matthew γέμει ἐξ ἁρπαγῆς. See *Oxford Studies,* p. 300.

49. ἡ σοφία τοῦ θεοῦ= God in His Providence. **A** Hebrew idea. See Proverbs viii. 22-31.

51. ἕως αἵματος Ζαχαρίου. See *Comm.*

Chap. xii. 1-12. This section appears in Matthew x. 26-33.
The two versions reveal considerable verbal
similarity. This, however, need not be taken to
indicate that the two editors derived this matter
from Q. St. Matthew may have had access to
St. Luke's special source. At any rate the peculiar
constructions of that source appear here.

1. ἤρξατο λέγειν. See note on iv. 21. προσέχετε
ἀπό. See also xx. 46.

6. ἐνώπιον τοῦ θεοῦ. See note on i. 6.

13-21. *The parable of the rich fool.*

19. εὐφραίνεσθαι. Does not appear in Matthew or
Mark, but it is found here, and also in xv. 23, 24,
29, 32, xvi. 19. In Acts ii. 26 it is used in a
quotation from Psalm xvi. 9.

22-34. *A discourse on trust in God.* This appears
also in Matthew vi. 25-33.

35-48. *A discourse on watchfulness and true service.*

32. For the phrase διδόναι τὴν βασιλείαν, see
Dalman, p. 134.

49-59. The effect of Christ's teaching and the signs
of the times.

50. βάπτισμα βαπτισθῆναι. See note on ii. 8. ἕως
ὅτου. So in xiii. 8, xv. 8, xxii. 16, xxiv. 49, all
from the special source.

Chap. xiii. 1-5. *Supposed judgment on Galilæans.*

1. παρῆσαν ἀπαγγέλλοντες. See note on i. 20.

2. παρά with acc. to express comparison, cf. xviii. 4.

6-9. *The barren fig-tree.*

10-17. *A woman is healed on the Sabbath Day.*

11. ἦν συνκύπτουσα. See note on i. 20.

16. θυγατέρα 'Αβραάμ. See note on i. 5.

11-21. *Two parables.*

22-35. *Conditions of admission to the Kingdom and
the lament over Jerusalem.*

26. ἐνώπιόν σου. See note on i. 6.

32. For this reference to Herod, see p. 163. The
lament over Jerusalem appears again in Matt. xxiii.
37-39. The editor of the first Gospel inserts it in

the section containing our Lord's denunciation of
the Scribes and Pharisees, as though it was spoken
in the Temple. St. Luke's source, however, gives it
as an incident of the journey towards Jerusalem.
The method of compiling the Logia followed in the
first Gospel makes it likely that the true historical
setting is to be found in the third Gospel.

Chap. xiv. 1-24. *Jesus in the Pharisee's house.*

    1. ἐγένετο ἐν τῷ ἐλθεῖν. See note on i. 1, 8. ἦσαν
    παρατηρούμενοι. See note on i. 20.
    3. νομικός. See note on vii. 30.
    10. ἐνώπιον. This word does not occur in Matt. or
    Mark, but is used twenty-four times by St. Luke,
    ἵνα with fut. Indic. Elsewhere at xx. 10 in Luke.
    25-35. *Conditions of Discipleship.*
    32. πρεσβείαν only twice in New Testament, both
    times in St. Luke's 'Travel Document.'

Chap. xv. 1-32. *Three parables.*

    1. διαγογγύζειν. Only here and xix.7 in New Testa-
    ment. Both passages belong to the special source.
    7. δίκαιος. Note the Jewish use of the word. Cf. i. 6,
    xiv. 14.
    10. and 18. Note the frequent use of ἐνώπιον. See
    i. 6. Note.

Chap. xvi. *The parable of the unjust steward.* This parable is
peculiar to the third Gospel.

    1. οἰκονόμος. This word occurs also in xii. 42, which
    belongs to this source. It occurs nowhere else in
    the Gospels. The Matthaean equivalent is δοῦλος.
    5. χρεοφειλέτης. See note on vii. 41.
    14-17. Jesus rebukes the Pharisees for covetousness.
    In this short section there occur several words and
    phrases peculiar to this source, such as δικαιοῦν
    (see note on vii. 29), ἐνώπιον and εὐκοπώτερον.
    18. *A pronouncement on divorce.*
    19-31. *The parable of the rich man and Lazarus.*
    22. ἐγένετο. See note on i. 5.

Chap. xvii. 1-10. Sundry discourses.

          11-19. The gratitude of the Samaritan leper. Another sympathetic reference to Samaritans. See p. 162.

          11-14. ἐγένετο ἐν τῷ with Infin. See note on i. 5. Dr. Stanton considers that this section was composed by St. Luke himself, the material for the story being taken from oral tradition. See p. 169.

          20-37. An Eschatological section.

          24. ἀστραπὴ ἀστράπτουσα. Cf. ii. 8, xi. 46, xxiii. 46.

Chap. xviii. 1-14. *Two parables.*

          5. παρέχειν κόπον. See note on xi. 7.

          9. ἐξουθενοῦντας. Cf. xxiii. 11.

Chap. xix. 1-10. *Zacchæus.*

          7. καταλῦσαι does not occur elsewhere in this sense except at ix. 12, a passage which comes from the same source.

          11-27. *The parable of the pounds.*

          11. This parable was spoken when the journey was nearly at an end.

          12. λαβεῖν ἑαυτῷ βασιλείαν. For the reference to the action of Herod, see the commentaries and supra, p. 163.

          15. καὶ ἐγένετο ἐν τῷ. See note on i. 5. In this section the words διεπραγματεύσαντο (15), αὐστηρός (21), and κατασφάξατε (27) are ἅπ. λεγ. in New Testament.

Chap. xxii. In this chapter occur several short sections which are peculiar to St. Luke, and many will have been derived from his special source and woven into the general fabric of Markan narrative. Such passages are vv. 14-18, 24-32, 33, 35-38, 43-44, 56-66, 70. Expressions characteristic of the source are ἐπιθυμίᾳ ἐπεθύμησα (15), ἕως ὅτου (16-18), διαμερίζεσθαι (17), οἱ ἀπόστολοι (14), στηρίζειν (32). v. 53 is Hebraic.

Chap. xxiii. In this chapter too there are passages taken from the source and interwoven with Markan matter.

Such passages are vv. 2, 4-5, 6-16, 19, 27-31, 33-38, 39-43, 46, 48-49, 54-56.

xxiii. 6-19. For the reference to Herod, see p. 163.

7. ἐξουσία in sense of jurisdiction. Not so used elsewhere.

8. ἦν θέλων. Note on i. 5.

9. γινόμενον of. miracles; also in iv. 23.

27-31. For the note of sympathy with women, see p. 163. For other features peculiar to the source in these sections note ἐνώπιον (14), ἐστὶν πεπραγμένον (15), τοῦ λαοῦ (27), ἄρξονται λέγειν (30). In v. 56 note that the women who prepared the spices for embalming the body of Jesus are said to be the same as those who had followed Him from Galilee. See note on viii. 3 and supra, p. 163.

Chap. xxiv. The Resurrection. The whole of this section was undoubtedly taken from the special source. For a discussion of the whole chapter see article in *Hibbert Journal*, 1905, by Torkild Skat Rördam, entitled *The Resurrection Appearances of Christ*. The chapter is closely connected linguistically with the Nativity section. The name of Joanna appears in v. 10 (see above, p. 164). Expressions which occur in the chapter and have already been commented on in these notes are :—τῇ δὲ μιᾷ τῶν σαββάτων (1), ἐγένετο ἐν τῷ κ.τ. λ. (4), καὶ ἰδού (4), ἦσαν πορευόμενοι (13), δυνατὸς ἐν λόγῳ ἐναντίον τοῦ θεοῦ καὶ λαοῦ (19), τὸν Ἰσραήλ . . . λυτροῦσθαι (21), ὤφθη (34).

In summing up the characteristics which we have sought to bring out in the preceding notes we would notice :

1. That a distinctly Hebraistic or Aramaic character belongs to every section which we have ascribed to St Luke's special source. The most prominent of these are (a) the use of ἐν τῷ with the infinitive mood of the verb which follows.

(b) The use of εἶναι with the present participle.

(c) The frequent employment of such words as ἐναντίον and ἐνώπιον. See note on i. 6.

(d) The use of such words and phrases as χάρις, εὐαγγελίζεσθαι, πρὸ προσώπου, ὁ λαός, θυγατὴρ Ἀβραάμ, βάπτισμα βαπτισθῆναι, νομικός, ἡλικία, κόπον παρέχειν, ἤρξατο λέγειν, κατακλίνεσθαι, κ.τ.λ. These are all to be found fairly distributed over the sections, and they are for the most part characteristic; that is, they are not found at all, or in some cases very slightly, in other sections of the three Gospels.

2. The references to Herod, found only in these sections and in several of them.

3. The references, always with some amount of sympathy, to the Samaritans. Nearly all of these occur in these sections.

4. The use of 'Ιουδαία for Palestine.

5. The womanly interest and point of view which is so marked as to give a character to the whole Gospel is to be found in these sections.

6. A Judaean tradition which is apparent in both the Nativity section and the closing section which records the appearances of our Lord after His resurrection.

It must be acknowledged that these are strongly marked characteristics, and when we find them, as we do, not in one or two of the sections, but fairly distributed over them all, they bind the different sections together into a certain unity of authorship. Such a unity may have been conferred by St. Luke himself, and it must be acknowledged that some of the characteristics, though not the most striking, occur in other sections of the Gospel, and also in Acts; but when we recall the strong Hebrew tendency which belongs to the whole of this part of the Gospel, it seems far more likely that they are to be attributed, not to the Gentile Luke, but to the source from which he derived the invaluable material embodied in this Gospel alone. That source must have been one to which St. Luke attached a very special value, for otherwise he would not have departed so frequently as he has done, especially in the closing incidents of our Lord's life which he records, from the Markan narrative, to which he is also indebted.

Dr. Stanton in an invaluable chapter on *Style in Luke's peculiar matter*, which I have used freely in compiling these notes, calls attention to these peculiarities of this Gospel, but demands, as indeed he shows, the greatest caution in drawing conclusions from them. On the whole he seems to incline towards ascribing their common characteristics to the editor rather than to his source, and he assigns to Luke himself the following sections, suggesting that the evangelist used an oral basis in compiling these narratives:—v. 1-11, vii. 36-50, viii. 1-3, x. 29-37, xvii. 11-19, xix. 41-44, xxiii. 5-12, 14-15, 39-43, and the whole of chapter xxiv. It is to be noticed that with the exception of two of these passages, they all belong to the group under consideration, and their differentiation from the rest of the Gospel gives them a certain unity, the recognition of which is, in our opinion, a distinct step in advance. Dr. Stanton seems to think that there is a certain amount of positive evidence of the use of a document, and we incline to the belief that this is greater both in quantity and in value than he is apparently inclined to allow. We also find it difficult to reconcile the statement that for these considerable and striking sections St. Luke had recourse to oral tradition, with the strong pronouncement against oral tradition, which Dr. Stanton makes elsewhere in his work. The advocates of oral tradition may well ask why, if the theory be allowed for these, it may not be allowed for other sections. Dr. Stanton closes his chapter with a note on the use of ἵνα, which we take the liberty of transcribing here, so conclusive does it seem to us in supporting the contention which we make in favour of a documentary, a single, and a unique source for all these portions of the third Gospel which we refer to a single source. Dr. Stanton says :

'The use of ἵνα by Luke seems to be of some significance in connection with the question of his use of a source, or sources, for his peculiar matter. In the Acts this particle occurs only twelve times, i.e. much less frequently in proportion than in any other New Testament writing, and very much less so than in most—and is for the most part not employed in an unclassical way. Turning to the third Gospel, we find that in Markan sections Luke (except at viii. 12, ix. 45, xx. 14) has used it only where Mark has it ; and further that he has several times avoided using it where Mark does ; while in another place (vii. 32) he so turns the sentence as to make the use of ἵνα less strange than it is in Mark. There are also a few instances in Logian passages, in two of which (Luke vi. 31, Matthew vii. 12, and Luke vii. 6, Matthew viii. 8) the use of ἵνα is, while in four others (iv. 3, vi. 34, xi. 33, 50) it may be derived from the source. When therefore we find ἵνα occurring twenty-two times in the peculiar matter in the third Gospel (viz. twice in chapters i. and ii., and twenty times in the peculiar passages subsequent to them), *i.e.* nearly half as many times again as in the whole of the Acts, one cannot but suspect that several of the instances, at least, were due to Luke's finding them in a source in which the particle was used more largely than he would of his own mind have been disposed to use it.'

EXCURSUS III

THE SAYINGS OF JESUS IN ST LUKE'S GOSPEL

The greater part of what is called ' the Sermon on the Mount' in the first Gospel appears in the third Gospel in two main divisions—vi. 17-49 and viii. 4-21. The chief differences between the two collections of sayings have been noted in chapter ii. It is also to be noted that many of the sayings which appear in the Matthaean collection are given by St. Luke as separate sayings uttered by Jesus on different occasions. These are found in greatest number in ' the Great Insertion,' or ' the Travel Document.' The following may serve as outstanding examples :

> Chap.   **x.** 5-7, 12, 13-15, 23.
>   **xi.** 1-4, 9-13, 14-28, 34-35.
>   **xii.** 2-9, 22-31, 33-34, 39-46, 51-53, 57-59.
>   **xiii.** 5, 20-21, 26-27, 34-35.
>   **xiv.** 5, 15-24, 26-27, 34-35.
>   **xv.** 3-7.
>   **xvi.** 13, 16-17.
>   **xvii.** 1, 23-24, 26-27, 30, 34-35.

Now this fact strongly supports the contention, made on pages 56-57, that these sayings did not come before the evangelists of the first and third Gospels in the form of some document in which the sayings had been already arranged in some sort of order, but that the two editors were entirely independent in this portion of their work. If St. Matthew dealt with some collection of sayings which he himself arranged according to a plan which commended itself to him, then we can understand how it is that he would place in the Sermon on the Mount such sayings as he considered belonged to that phase of his Master's teaching which he was anxious to preserve, whether they were spoken early or late in the course of that Master's ministry. St. Luke working on quite a different plan, and finding the sayings embodied in the record of the journey of Jesus from Galilee to Jerusalem, would give them as they appeared in his source. Dr. Willoughby Allen in his analysis of the Logian document, used by the editor of the first Gospel, comments upon some of these sayings as recorded by St. Luke, and says that they did not stand in the Sermon on the Mount, or St. Luke would have placed them in vi. 17-49 or viii. 4-21. To the present writer it seems a more likely explanation that the Sermon on the Mount is a collocation of sayings made by St. Matthew, and that the difference between the two Gospels in this particular is to be accounted for as above. So again Dr. Allen in commenting upon Matthew v. 18-19 says that this is 'unsuitably placed' in the sermon, but the lack of coherence on which Dr. Allen bases this remark is to be explained as due to the character of St. Matthew's source, and the method upon which he worked. The same explanation accounts for the position of Matthew v. 25 (cf. Luke xii. 57-59). 'The connection in the Sermon is artificial and literary,' says Dr. Allen. Such a comment is correct if we suppose that there was any great amount of coherence between the sayings as they came before St. Matthew, but the 'literary' character of the connection is quite in keeping with the method of St. Matthew as we conceive it.

CHAPTER VII

THE JUSTIFICATION OF HISTORICAL CRITICISM

THE study of Gospel Origins is not an end in itself.   It is after all only a preliminary study.   But it is a study which is absolutely necessary if the Christian is to arrive at the full assurance of faith.   We shall indeed begin with our personal experience of Christ, but if we are to know the certainty of those things wherein we have been instructed we must consider the historical records which account for the experience ;   we are bound to ask ourselves whether they possess sufficient authority to enable us to give a reason for the faith that is in us.   The problems raised by the Gospels merely as literature are of sufficiently engrossing interest, but it is not from the literary point of view that we claim urgency for the many questions which we have been considering.   The whole religious position of the Christian depends ultimately upon whether the facts of the Gospel story can be guaranteed.   Christianity depends upon revelation, and this is subjective in the experience of the believer, but objective in facts of history. The revelation of the Risen Lord lacks definiteness unless it can be related to the human life of Jesus, and the history of the record of that life assumes an importance which can never be exaggerated as soon as this is clearly seen.   We shall be neither surprised nor impatient when the question of miracle forces itself again and again upon our attention ; for the Resurrection of our Lord from the dead is central in the Christian faith, and in view of that Resurrection the question of other miraculous works becomes entirely secondary.   The general question of miracles is before us

again, and we shall show presently how impossible it is
to discuss that question without raising other questions
which have to do with the fact of authorship, and with
the circumstances under which the writings which record
those miracles were composed. It will also be seen that
any attempt to argue either for or against the fact of
miracle is doomed to failure whenever the argument
rests upon mere presupposition with reference to Gospel
sources.

But the question of miracles does not stand alone. It is
after all only a part of a far larger question, and this is
what has been happily called ' the Fact of Christ.' The
Person of our Lord is the glowing centre round which the
highest human thought revolves. It is in Him that we
see the Father. It is in Him that we have our redemption,
and in Him stands our hope of eternal life. The Gospels
are so many attempts to set before men the fact and the
interpretation of that Personality. They contain the
witness of Jesus to Himself, and the testimony of those
who have declared that which they saw with their eyes,[1]
that which they contemplated with a vision which
deepened as they peered into the depth beyond the depth,
and that which their hands handled in the sacred
ministries of love and fellowship.

The Personality of Jesus is being considered to-day
from two different points of view, and we mention these
not with the intention of discussing them so much as to
make good the claim with which we are here concerned—
that in neither case can the positions taken up by the
different schools be made good unless the foundation is
first laid in establishing the value of the Gospels as historical
documents. The idealist would abandon the Gospels
altogether. It is true that he derives from them some
vague concept of Christ, but he attaches little value to
the history. That which is of supreme importance for

[1] 1 John i. 1.

him is the entirely subjective experience of which he is
conscious.

There is another school consisting of those who confine
their attention to what they are pleased to call ' History.'
They begin by emptying the record of all that goes beyond
the range of common human experience, and they seek
to account for the Personality of our Lord on the ground
of His environment, social, intellectual, and religious.
To them He was the product of His age, and beyond that
they do not go. The fact that the age in which He lived
witnessed the rise of what has become known as ' the
Apocalyptic Method ' is sufficient to enable them to explain
whatever reference to transcendent life and power may
appear in our Lord's witness to Himself. Here again we
shall endeavour to show that before any measure of
finality can appear in the conclusions arrived at in this
matter, the history of the documents upon which the
argument is based needs the fullest consideration. We
shall endeavour to deal briefly with each of these points
in the remainder of this chapter.

Appeals are constantly being made for and against a
belief in miracles on the ground of historical criticism of
the Gospels which record them. It is, of course, the only
sound method of dealing with the question. To begin
with the laying down of an axiom that ' miracles do not
happen ' is to beg the whole question at issue. We are
not then surprised to find that in a recent work on miracles
the argument is based mainly upon historical criticism
of the Synoptic Gospels. Mr. J. M. Thompson [1] bases the
greater part of his contention upon such facts as we have
discussed in preceding chapters ; but it is to be questioned
whether he does not take too much for granted, and whether
he is justified in drawing the conclusions with which he
presents us. He says that St. Mark knows nothing of
the Virgin Birth, and he concludes that the evidence for

[1] *Miracles in the New Testament.*

this event is considerably weakened in consequence. He also assumes that the second Gospel is composite ; that it contains in addition to the Petrine tradition a considerable amount which was derived from Q, as well as from other sources. He then shows that by far the greater number of miracles belong to the Petrine tradition. He further divides this last into two sections, one describing a Galilean and the other a Judaean ministry, and shows that in the latter there is no record of miraculous works done by our Lord. He then asks how it is that no miracles were wrought in hostile Judaea but only in friendly Galilee. The implication in this somewhat rhetorical question is perfectly obvious. It is to discount the evidence for miracles.

We do not of course discuss the general question,[1] or attempt to value the evidence for or against the historicity of the record in this chapter. Our one contention is that Mr. Thompson's conclusions rest upon assumptions, and as the great body of modern scholars are unable to accept his presuppositions, his argument carries no weight with them, though it may seriously prejudice the minds of those who have not been able to consider the critical questions involved. To take the points just mentioned in inverse order, we notice that no argument against miracles can be based with any fairness upon the fact that they are more frequent in the earlier part of the Markan record than they are in the latter. That record is almost entirely descriptive of the Galilean ministry of our Lord. For some reason or other—and it is by no means difficult to suggest a reason—St. Peter chose to limit his account of our Lord's ministry to that portion of it which was accomplished in Galilee ; and St. Mark follows St. Peter closely, as internal evidence as well as tradition assures us. According to St. Peter, then, our Lord visited Jerusalem only to die. That He had preached in Judaea, and had

[1] See *Miracles: An Outline of the Christian View*, by the Rev. F. Platt.

in the course of His ministry worked miracles, we know from the fourth Gospel; but as Mr. Thompson holds that this Gospel ' cannot be treated as a historically true account of the miracles of Christ,' we shall not labour the point. For our purpose the fourth Gospel may be left entirely out of account, though modern scholars are coming to see that for minuteness and accuracy of historical detail the fourth Gospel is superior to the Synoptic account. But even in the latter there are indications that the evangelists knew of a Judaean ministry, and in the many spaces left uncovered by the Synoptic tradition there is room for a Judaean ministry. If these evangelists chose to limit their accounts to the occasion when our Lord was crucified, the absence of miracle on such an occasion is without significance so far as the historical evidence for miracles is concerned. The absence of such mighty works cannot be used to support an argument that the appearance of miracles in the record is due to the simple and superstitious imagination of the peasants of Galilee.

With reference to Q Mr. Thompson concludes that while this document is the only rival to the Petrine memoirs of St. Mark as an early and good authority, it contains no evidence for miracles. But here again Mr. Thompson bases his argument upon a pure assumption. In all the criticism of the Synoptic Gospels there is no question more disputed than that of the contents of Q. If the arguments advanced in preceding chapters have any weight it may fairly be argued that the document so designated contained no narrative whatever, and that it consisted of sayings of Jesus with the minimum of intro-ductory matter intended merely to serve as connections between one saying and another. To make the absence of miracles from writings which had nothing to do with them an argument against miracles generally is not a method to be commended in any department of literary criticism.

It is of course open to any one to say that the view of Q
advanced in this work is not to be accepted, but even if
Harnack's reconstruction of Q be followed, as it is confessedly
by Mr. Thompson, the fact should not have been ignored
that Harnack himself says of Q that ' it was in no sense
a biographical narrative, but essentially a collection of
discourses.' It is true that in spite of that statement
Harnack includes the miracle of the healing of the
centurion's servant in his reconstructed Q, but his incon-
sistency in doing so has often been pointed out. It is
quite clear that whether we accept Harnack's, or any
other reconstruction of Q, we cannot argue against miracles
on the ground that they do not appear in that document.
But we are quite prepared, if needs be, to argue for miracles
even from Q. For while it contains no account of miracle,
it does present us with the fact that our Lord in many of
His discourses takes the fact that He had done such works
for granted, and bases His arguments upon the fact.
He assumed that His miraculous works were matters
of common knowledge.

The same weakness in Mr. Thompson's method of
criticism appears again when he comes to discuss the
greatest miracle of all—the Resurrection of our Lord from
the dead. We are told that ' the witness of St. Matthew
and St. Luke is conditioned by their habit of editing
Mark without fresh evidence according to certain *a
priori* tendencies ; that when they are drawing on new
sources of information they are probably (with the
exception of Q) less trustworthy than Mark.' With reference to St. Mark's evidence Mr. Thompson goes on to
tell us that he gives no account of the actual Resurrection,
' his account breaks off without describing any Resurrection appearances, but not before it has hinted—partly
by its very reaction against this view—that the apostles'
story of the appearances, not the women's story of the
empty tomb, was the original and central ground of belief

in the Resurrection.' It is difficult to take such statements seriously. The veriest tyro in Textual Criticism
knows that the abrupt ending of the second Gospel is due
to the mutilation of a manuscript. It would be a curious
piece of composition which ' broke off ' with the words
ἐφοβοῦντο γάρ, and in view of this to speak of St. Mark's
account as one which ' breaks off without describing any
Resurrection appearances,' and then to imply from this
that St. Mark felt a mental reaction against the women's
story of the empty tomb, and that the evidence from the
second Gospel in favour of the Resurrection is thereby
impaired, is false criticism and false reasoning. The
account of the Resurrection in Matthew follows that in the
second Gospel so closely, up to the point where the break
in the text of the latter occurs, that we may feel a reasonable amount of confidence that the true conclusion of
the second Gospel is to be discovered in the first. Mr.
Thompson writes as though the account of the Resurrection
in the first Gospel was the work of St. Matthew, but if
there is one thing in the whole range of Gospel criticism
which has received anything like a consensus of opinion
it is that the narrative portion of the first Gospel is Markan
in origin. Where additional details appear in the first
Gospel, it is quite possible that these are due, not to
editing on the part of St. Matthew, but to the fact that
an earlier edition of the Markan narrative was used by the
unknown evangelist who adds that narrative to the
Matthaean Logia, and thus composed the first Gospel as
we have it.

Why should it be assumed that where St. Luke
draws from other sources they are less trustworthy than
St. Mark ? We are told that the latter did not himself
follow Jesus. His record consists of so much of the
facts recounted by St. Peter as he remembered. There is
room in this for more than one explanation of omissions
from the Markan narrative. But St. Luke's source for

this section of the third Gospel—even if we do not accept
that he derived it from one of the very women who visited
the tomb and found it empty—reveals a great knowledge
of detail introduced incidentally and without the slightest
straining after effect, and we may well conclude that this
evidence is derived at first hand, and from one who was
apparently an eye-witness of what is described. If then
we are to choose between the two sources—and we have
yet to discover any real contradiction between them—
the balance would seem to incline towards the Lukan
rather than the Markan source.

In dealing with the story of the Virgin Birth Mr.
Thompson reveals a method of criticism in which we
cannot follow him. St. Mark's account of our Lord's
ministry, after the very briefest introduction describing
the Baptism, begins in Galilee. To argue from the absence
of all reference to our Lord's life prior to this event that
St. Mark knows nothing of the Virgin Birth is an outstanding example of that *argumentum a silentio* which,
one might have thought, has been sufficiently discredited.
We have discussed these conclusions of Mr. Thompson
not at all in order to weigh the evidence for or against the
facts which he discusses, but solely to show how absolutely
necessary it is to have before us some clear and intelligent
account of the origins of the Synoptic Gospels if we wish
to draw conclusions from these records of events. No
argument based upon the history of the records can carry
conviction unless we first deal with the questions of
authorship, and of the circumstances attending the com-
positions of the writings. Mr. Thompson bases his conclusions upon ' criticism,' but it is precisely on the critical
side that his arguments are most unsound, and the same
result must follow upon every attempt to argue from the
record without first determining as far as possible the
sources from which that record was drawn.

But the question of miracles is not the only one before

us in the present day.   Dr. Schweitzer and others have
brought into prominence the question of Apocalypse as
affording an explanation of prominent features of the Gospel
story, and this question too must be examined in the light of
Gospel origins in so far as these can be ascertained.   The
Gospels which have come down to us are literary documents, and they were written in an age in which what we
call ' Apocalyptic Literature ' was in vogue.   Our Lord's
words and much of His teaching show that He also
followed this method of expressing Himself.   Whether
He did so within limits, or was ' a thoroughgoing
Eschatologist,' does not enter into the reference of this
work.[1]   But the analysis of such eschatological passages
as appear in the Gospels can scarcely be attempted apart
from the prior question of Gospel sources.   As to the fact
that our Lord used the language of Apocalypse we may
refer briefly to the considerable section which we have in
Mark xiii., a section which is reproduced in Matthew xxiv.
and Luke xxi.   There are also shorter passages in which
the idea, though really dominant, is only implied.   Such
passages, for instance, as Mark viii. 38 and Mark xiv. 62
can be interpreted only in the light of ' Apocalypse.'
These ideas are also prominent in not a few of our Lord's
parables.   The Parables of the Ten Virgins, the Tares,
the Ten Talents, and most of those relating to ' the Kingdom
of Heaven ' are distinctly Apocalyptic in character.   But
even more significant than these are the many words and
phrases so frequently on the lips of Jesus.   Such are
' The Son of Man,' ' The Kingdom of Heaven,' ' The End
of the World—or Age.'   Such phrases can only be considered in the light of their use in the literature which
preceded and which followed the days of our Lord's
ministry.

The significance of the ' Little Apocalypse ' in Mark xiii.

[1] On the general question the writer may be allowed to refer the reader to
his Fernley Lecture entitled *Christ and the Gospels*, chap. vi.

with references to Gospel sources has been already discussed in chapter v., and we need do no more here than
refer the reader to what has been already written.   But
the fact that Apocalyptic writing appears in both the
Markan and the Logian documents has led some to consider
whether there is not to be detected a heightening of effect
in the expressions used in later writings when compared
with those used in earlier.   Thus in a valuable appendix
to the *Oxford Studies in the Synoptic Problem* we find
Mr. Streeter speaking of ' an evolution of eschatological
conceptions from the present spiritual conception of the
Kingdom in Q, through Mark, to Matthew.'   In Q while
the catastrophic eschatology is undoubtedly present, it
is vague and undefined.   Mark belongs to the transitional
stage.   Matthew further elaborates the eschatological
element, and emphasises its Apocalyptic side.   He even
shows ' a tendency to omit sayings inconsistent with the
view of the kingdom as future and catastrophic.'   The
passages upon which Mr. Streeter bases this differentiation
must be duly weighed by the student of the Gospels.   We
can here discuss only the general question in the light of
Gospel sources, and of their relation to one another.   From
this point of view we would say that any argument based
upon the relation of these sources to one another in time
must always be precarious.   We do not know that the
second Gospel, as we have it, preceded the first.   As we
have shown above there are many features of the Markan
narrative which indicate that the version of this which
appears in the first Gospel was prior to that which we have
in the second.   The argument from Q also is uncertain.
We do not know when the compilation of sayings used by
St. Matthew was made, or to what extent they took their
present form by reason of the interpretative method of
those who compiled them.   It is quite possible that
Logia were added to the collection subsequently to St.
Mark's episcopacy in Egypt, during which he wrote down

for the Church in that country his memoirs of St. Peter's preaching.   But apart from such considerations we may well ask whether the true order of development was not more likely to be one in which the more ' catastrophic ' features of the ' Parousia ' would appear in the earlier rather than in the later writings.   We know that St. Paul's view of the Parousia, as it appears in the Corinthian Epistles, differs from that which he describes in his first Epistle to the Thessalonians, and every year which passed would lead the Church to see that the view which it held at first of the coming of the Lord in power and in the glory of the Father needed modification.   It would be led to interpret His sayings more and more as declarations of great, moral, and spiritual effects, and it is just the later writings which would reveal this tendency.

To the present writer it seems a sounder method of criticism to abandon all attempts at chronological sequence in such matters.   It is difficult to decide what was the chronological order of the Gospels as we have them, and it is still more difficult to say exactly when this source or that was composed.   It is better to content ourselves with what should find a ready acceptance—that our Lord used the language of His days, and would thus adopt a phraseology which might suggest to His hearers a catastrophic interpretation, passing as it would do through minds that had been trained to take that view of the coming of the Son of Man.   But though He used the words He filled them with a new content.   He laid the emphasis where those who preceded Him had failed to lay it.   His teaching contained the germ of that which went far beyond the social and political dreams of Jewish Apocalypse.   The truth was greater than the phrase which held it, and only slowly have men come to see—if haply even now they see—the fuller content of revelation, and the unfolding of that mystery which is Christ in us, the hope of glory.

Eschatology is, as we have said, only a point of view from which the attempt may be made to account for the effect which the Personality of our Lord has produced upon human thought and life, and side by side with this attempt to account for Christ as the natural product of an age possessing marked historical characteristics we have the many attempts that are being made to offer to the world an individualistic interpretation of the same Personality. To many minds religion is independent of all revelation on the plane of human history. No longer are the Scriptures searched because they testify of Jesus. Impressions, often conditioned by aesthetic or philosophic considerations alone, make up all that is required in the sphere of religion ; and it is the easiest thing in the world for a new cult to be started, and to attract a considerable number of followers, if the new apostle is sufficiently startling in his method or in himself to challenge attention. This is due very largely to a fact which is not in itself to be deplored. It is the result of the modern emphasis upon experience as authoritative in religion. The age in which dogma held the first place, and the acceptance of a creed was considered to be an adequate response to its pronouncements, has passed or is rapidly passing away. In place of dogma men are turning to schemes of morals, which may be individual, social, or political. Others surrender themselves to a still more subjective expression of faith. The formula of acceptance which the individual Christian keeps before himself in judging of the acceptability of any form of religion is ' That which finds me.' It is the moral or psychological significance of faith which seems to be most prominent at the present moment. The uncertainty which gathers around everything which has to do with a document—whether that document records the facts of history, or the interpretation of those facts—has led to a general impatience with any presentation of the Christian faith in which the intellectual element is at all prominent. This tendency is not to be wholly regretted. The emphasis laid upon creed too often favoured a lessening of the moral content of spiritual life, and the contrast was at once set up between ' forms of faith ' and a life which was ' in the right.' Such a contrast should never have arisen. The two are not mutually exclusive. Indeed it is becoming clearer every day that the one can scarcely exist without the other, and that one should thus be pitted against the other is the result of that exaggeration in emphasis which apparently we never learn to avoid. At any rate the fact remains that this contrast has been set up, and where this takes place the vote is given in favour of the moral life.

It was inevitable too that this same intellectual emphasis should bring faith into comparison with those logical processes which belong to the school of science, and as soon as the latter began to appeal to the thought and imagination of men a spirit of antagonism between the two began to make itself felt. This antagonism also, like that between morals and faith, never possessed any real ground, and this is happily being realised both on the side of science and on that of religion. But where it existed the science which dealt with phenomena governed by fixed and unvarying laws seemed more definite and more final in its conclusions than that which moved in the realm of faith, and it was accordingly preferred. In so far as this revolt from religion indicates merely a protest against the excessive intellectualism which produced this false antagonism it is to be approved rather than deplored. But as is always the case, the reaction has been carried to an extreme, and the period in which agnosticism was prevalent has been followed by one in which pure subjectivity threatens to become the accepted basis of faith. Esoteric systems— often advanced by irresponsible individuals—Theosophies, and different forms of Christian Science, have come into vogue, and the number of those who hold one or other

of these with more or less of conviction must be considerable. We refer to them merely to illustrate the perils
which threaten any undue emphasis upon personal
experience apart from a revelation in history, as a basis
for religion. They are all perversions of an individual
expression of faith which has not been corrected by the
presentation in history of the true foundations of faith.

For while it is true that the Christian faith is more than
the Christian creed, it is impossible to dispense altogether
with the objective element in religion. It is true that
religion is to be found in the impact of one personality
upon another—the divine upon the human—and in the
response of the human to the divine, but we cannot afford
to ignore the revelation in history through which that
impact has become definite and complete in the consciousness of man. The true corrective—indeed the only
corrective—to the fancies and extravagances of subjective
faith is to be found in the interpretation of the history
which has come down to us. We need to verify and con-
firm the experience by the recorded fact. We are always
in peril of reducing religion to a superstition, and if we
would avoid the danger we must find in the Gospels the
delineation of the causes which account for the spiritual
assurance, and which alone lead it to its full development.
The important thing is indeed the revelation—the content
of the Gospels rather than the means by which it reaches
us, but if we are to know the certainty concerning the
things in which we have been instructed, we are bound to
scrutinise the record by which alone we can assure ourselves
that we have not followed cunningly devised fables.

The Gospels present us with the history-basis of a
great spiritual revelation ; we must ask ourselves what
credentials they have to offer. The process of doing so
entails a mental discipline, from which many shrink in
these days of hasty work and superficial investigation, but
we must admit that the burden is laid with even greater

weight upon our spirits, and we cannot do justice to the capacities of our spiritual nature unless we justify the tremendous claim with which these Gospels present us. The confusion, to say nothing of the moral weakness which follows upon any neglect to consider these historical documents, has been well expressed by a great German scholar and critic, and we shall not apologise for the length of the passage which we quote from his writings. Harnack, speaking of the present situation in Gospel criticism, says :

' Men soar away into sublime discussions concerning the meaning of " the kingdom of God," " the Son of Man," " Messiahship," etc., and with problems of genuineness in the light of " higher " criticism ; while the lower problems, whose treatment involves real scavenger's work in which one is almost choked in dust, are passed by on the other side. Or where this is not the case, the investigation is still never carried far enough, it breaks off prematurely, and the critic rests satisfied with work only half done. Hence the wretched plight in which the criticism of the Gospels finds itself in these days. . . . This wretched state is apparent above all in the case of those who are compelled to take their knowledge of the criticism of the New Testament at second hand, or have condemned themselves to this unassuming intellectual position. They are like reeds swaying with the blasts of the most extreme and mutually exclusive hypotheses, and find everything which is offered them in this connection " very worthy of consideration." To-day they are ready to believe that there was no such person as Jesus, while yesterday they regarded Him as a neurotic visionary shown to be such with convincing force by His own words, if only these are rightly interpreted, which words, by the way, have been excellently transmitted by tradition. To-morrow He has become for them an Essene, as may be proved like-wise from His own words ; and yet the day before yesterday

none of those words were His own ; and perhaps on the
very same day it was accounted correct to regard Him as
belonging to some Greek sect of esoteric gnostics—a sect
which still remains to be discovered, and which with its
symbols and sacraments represented a religion of a
chaotic and retrograde character, nay, exercised a
beneficial influence upon the development of culture. Or
rather He was an anarchist monk like Tolstoi, or still
better, a genuine Buddhist, who had, however, come
under the influence of ideas originating in ancient Babylon,
Persia, Egypt, and Greece ; or, better still, He was the
eponymous hero of the mildly revolutionary and
moderately radical fourth estate in the capital of the
Roman world. It is evident, forsooth, that He may
possibly have been all of these things, and may be assumed
to have been one of them. If, therefore, one only keeps
hold of all these reins, naturally with a loose hand, one is
shielded from the reproach of not being up to date, and
this is more important by far than the knowledge of the
facts themselves, which indeed do not so much concern
us, seeing that in this twentieth century we must of course
wean ourselves from a contemptible dependence upon
history in matters of religion ' (*The Sayings of Jesus*,
Intro. p. xiii.).

The sarcasm in this statement is sharp, but most of
those who have considered the matter will acknowledge
that it is deserved. There is no question in religion of
such supreme importance as that of the fact of Christ,
and the significance of that fact for men. For the discovery
of these things we are dependent upon our own experience
in the light of certain documents. The history of these
documents, then, how they came into being, the relation
of one writer to the other, and the point of view from
which each writer wrote, these things are of the first
importance, and yet they are left to only a few. The
greater number of these are content with a very partial

investigation, on the strength of which they make the most elaborate, the most destructive, theories, to the distress and often the religious loss of those who cannot verify their data.

What then may we claim to be accredited results in criticism ?   What balance may we strike between losses and gains in the critical method of dealing with the Gospel records ?   In former days we used to speak of ' a threefold evidence,' and of ' a triple tradition.'   Such phrases became current when the three Gospels were thought to be independent of one another.   They implied a narrative which had come to us along three distinct lines, and had emanated from three distinct sources.   Where the accounts given showed correspondence, it was felt that the evidence was peculiarly strong.   At the mouth of two or three witnesses every word might be established.   But as soon as it became evident that the Gospels were not independent, but that each contained matter which, even in details of expression, belonged also to the other two, it became necessary to abandon such expressions or to use them in another sense.   The latter course was taken by Dr. E. A. Abbott,[1] who used the phrase ' triple tradition ' for ' those words and phrases which are common to Matthew, Mark, and Luke.'   But in more recent days it has been seen that the phrase cannot be used with this meaning.   For critical study of Gospel sources has shown that where such words and phrases occur the linguistic correspondence is often due to the fact that the writings were taken from a common source.   It is now generally accepted that the first and third evangelists have embodied in their Gospels whole blocks of narrative which, if not taken directly from the second Gospel, are distinctly Markan in origin.   Where such correspondences occur we have not a triple tradition but a single tradition, and at first sight it would appear that there had been in consequence some loss of corro-

---

[1] *Encylo. Brit., sub verb.* ' Gospels.'

borative evidence in consequence. In the same way the
' double tradition ' which was found in the sayings of our
Lord recorded in both Matthew and Luke is, as a phrase,
open to objection on the part of those who hold that one
evangelist embodied in his Gospel that which had appeared
in the writings of his predecessor, or that each had recourse
to a common collection which was prior to both of theirs.
In this case, too, the tradition would be really single, in the
sense that the two records emanated from the same source.
We have seen that probably there is more to be said in
favour of this double tradition than could be said in favour
of the triple ; for opinion inclines to the belief that St.
Luke and St. Matthew derived their discourses of our Lord
from two independent collections of Logia.[1]

It must of course always be understood that where one
evangelist has embodied the writings of his predecessor
in his own work, there has been no attempt at deception,
collusion, or literary dishonesty. He would do so, we
may feel sure, because in his opinion the account was
authoritative, and if we believe that the influence of the
Spirit of truth rested upon him in this process of selection,
as it had rested upon his predecessor in recording this or
that incident in the life of our Lord, though there may not
be a triple tradition there is nevertheless a triple authority
for the incident as having approved itself to three independent evangelists. But the fact is that this loss of
corroborative evidence is only in appearance, and we
may see that in an incident or saying which appears in
the three strata, which run through the Gospel narrative,
we have our threefold tradition not merely restored but
given now in a form which is divested of the many uncertainties which belonged to the former view of the
Gospels, and resting upon a more assured historical basis.
For we may now feel confident that we have in the three
Gospels first of all a common Markan narrative. This is

[1] See p. 56.

generally acknowledged to rest upon a source more authoritative than St. Mark himself. The latter may be responsible for details of phraseology, and it is probable that he has inserted here and there a section which rests upon his own authority and experience ; but by far the greatest amount of the Markan narrative is acknowledged to be Petrine in origin, and the statement, preserved for us by Eusebius, that St. Mark wrote down what St. Peter was in the habit of saying to his hearers is seen to be intrinsically correct. In the Markan narrative then we are able to go behind St. Mark to the great advantage of the record in the matter of authority. In the chapters which precede this an attempt has been made to show that the original memoirs of St. Peter's preaching were enriched by the addition of incidents from the same source. These are therefore as authentic as the first, and all tend to heighten the effect of that great Personality whom St. Peter portrayed to the early Church.

There is less agreement among modern critics with reference to the second source, but it is a distinct gain on the side of the Discourse Document that we now have this clearly distinguished from the Markan narrative. Scholars differ as to the nature and contents of Q, but all are agreed that this document is other than that which is most fully expressed in the second Gospel ; and, though the authority of St. Matthew cannot be claimed for the whole of the first Gospel, yet it is certain that his contribution is incorporated in that Gospel, and that it must be sought in that part of it which records the discourses of Jesus. Here then we are able to recover the double tradition as we have recovered the triple. For when we find the teaching of Jesus given in connection with some incident in Mark and again in the form of a separate Logian in Matthew, or —as sometimes happens—in the narrative section and also in the discourses of the first Gospel, we have undoubtedly a doubly authenticated record, and the authority of St.

Matthew may be added to that of St. Peter in the Markan narrative.

As we have shown in preceding chapters, scholars are uncertain whether St. Luke derived the sayings recorded by him from the same source as that which St. Matthew used. Most critics agree that he has done so, and this common source is that which has been designated by the formula Q. But there is an increasing opinion that the differences between the sayings in the one Gospel and those in the other are too great to justify this belief in a common source, and if this opinion becomes established we shall secure another authority for sayings which appear in the three Gospels. For though St. Luke was not an apostle, as St. Peter and St. Matthew were, yet we cannot doubt that he too was guided in his selection of those deeds and words which he has recorded. There is no small measure of inspiration to be found in the work of the evangelist who has preserved for us the Parable of the Prodigal Son.

There remains the considerable section which contains matter peculiar to the third Gospel. Opinions as to the source or sources of this section are many and varied ; but whatever its source may be there can be no two opinions as to its value. It may be described as being in itself a Gospel—a Gospel of Love and Forgiveness. It begins with the life of the Holy Family, and all the wonder of the revelation made to her who was indeed ' blessed among women,' and it closes with the revelation to loving hearts of the Risen Lord, and of His return to the bosom of the Father. All through the intervening chapters there runs the golden thread of Christ's compassion for outcast Jew and alien Samaritan, and His gentle and reverent dealing with needy womanhood. It is the Gospel which tells us of joy in heaven for the penitent, and of a place in the Father's house for Lazarus the beggar, and for Zacchæus the publican. Whoever may have

furnished this record there is no mistaking the note of
inspiration in it.   St. Luke obtained the priceless story
from one who saw and heard the Master, and had the
insight of love and the quick intuition which enabled one,
who was probably the earliest of all the evangelists, to
record that which the world could never afford to lose.
The influence of the Spirit which gave St. Luke the unerring
instinct of a true discrimination led him to select this
material for insertion in his Gospel.   Here too we may
claim authority for the record, an authority which belongs
to St. Luke, and in equal measure to his source.

This present study of writings, which contain what
the human mind will never exhaust, draws to its appointed
close.   Fidelity to the increasing light given to men, in
fulfilment of the promise that through the ministry of
the Spirit of truth we shall be led into all the truth, has
caused us to see that other writings stand behind the
Gospels we have been considering, and that we can only
understand the relation of these Gospels to one another
in so far as we take into account the sources from which
they sprang.   To some it may seem that such an analysis
is fraught with peril.   They tremble for the ark of God.
They fear that such Gospels, precious to them beyond all
that words can express, may lose the authority which
their own spiritual experience has told them belongs to
the words which are spirit and life.   To all such we would
say that no criticism of human words can affect the fact
which those words seek to express.   It is the living Christ
who has brought new life to the Christian, and he must
beware lest, in his anxiety for the letter, he exalt this last
to a place which belongs to the Christ Himself.   But we
would claim that to the humble and the devout seeker
after truth any attempt to see more clearly what part
the human element has played in the production and the
preservation of these Scriptures only helps him to see more
clearly that in which the hope of all the world resides—

the Person of our Lord and Saviour Jesus Christ. Indeed, the wonder grows when we consider that which emerges from the many and varied parts which make up the whole of the Christian record. Men and women, some known some unknown, have brought into that record their several recollections of what their Master wrought, and what were the words which fell from His lips. Their recollection has been exposed to the common weakness of all that is human. Their impressions have been coloured by their own peculiar spiritual and mental condition to which that Master appealed, through which indeed they came to see Him as He was. But out of all these varied elements, as the final result of all these processes, there has emerged the wonder of a Personality infinite in significance, meeting the differing needs of a world of men, and yet single and complete. There is no incongruity between the picture drawn by one evangelist and the picture drawn by another. It is one Lord Jesus Christ who is the heart of the Gospels, however many those may be who have taken in hand to draw up a narrative.

The unquestioned cause of this wondrous unity is to be discovered in Him who is the spring and source of inspiration. For there rested upon the eager-hearted fisherman, telling to some group of simple souls what Jesus did, the directing Spirit of truth. With equal force, with a like immediacy, that same Spirit guided and governed the young man who listened to the preacher, and wrote down all he could remember of what the preacher said. Away in humble homes men spoke of what the Master said; gentle women recalled His wondrous grace, and over their meditations the same Spirit brooded creating the one impression, framing the one figure which was to command the adoration of the world. Later on the Church took up the work. This evangelist or that set himself to select what was worthy to abide, and to discard the manifold accretions which threatened to conceal or to disfigure. Later still in the councils of the Church men considered what books should be accepted as sacred Scriptures, as the Gospel of the living God. Over their deliberations the same Holy Spirit presided, and because of His continued ministry we discover to-day in the Gospels this marvellous unity of thought and purpose, and stand face to face at last with one Person human and divine, in knowledge of whom standeth our eternal life.

> ' Here is a tale of things done ages since ;
>   What truth was ever told the second day ?
>   Wonders that would prove doctrine, go for nought ;
>   Remains the doctrine, love : Well, we must love ;
>   And what we love most, power and love in one,
>   Let us acknowledge on the record here,
>   Accepting these in Christ.'

BIBLIOGRAPHY

Synopsis of the Gospels in Greek, by Dr. Arthur Wright.

Horae Synopticae, by the Rev. Sir J. C. Hawkins.

The Gospels as Historical Documents, by Dr. V. H. Stanton.

Studies in the Synoptic Problem, by Members of the University of Oxford.

An Introduction to the New Testament, by Dr. T. Zahn.

An Introduction to the Literature of the New Testament, by Dr. J. Moffat.

Principles of Lit. Crit. and the Synoptic Problem, by Dr. E. De Witt Burton.

The Beginnings of Gospel Story, by Dr. B. W. Bacon.

The Gospel History and its Transmission, by Dr. Burkitt.

The Sayings of Jesus, by Dr. Adolf Harnack.

The Common Tradition of the Synoptic Gospels, by Dr. E. A. Abbott and Mr. W. G. Rushbrooke.

An Introduction to the Synoptic Problem, by Rev. E. R. Buckley.

Articles on Matthew, Mark, Luke, Logia and Gospels, etc., in *The Dictionary of the Bible* (Hastings); *The Encyclopedia Biblica* (Cheyne).

INDEX

Studies in Theology

A New Series of Hand-books, being aids to interpretation
in Biblical Criticism for the use of Ministers,
Theological Students and general readers.

12mo, cloth. 75 cents net per volume.

THE aim of the series is described by the general title.
It is an attempt to bring all the resources of modern
learning to the interpretation of the Scriptures, and
to place within the reach of all who are interested
the broad conclusions arrived at by men of distinction in the
world of Christian scholarship on the great problems of Faith
and Destiny. The volumes are critical and constructive, and
their value can scarcely be overstated. Each volume will
contain bibliographies for the guidance of those who wish to
pursue more extended studies.

The writers selected for the various volumes are represen-
tative scholars both in this country and in Europe. Each of
them has been assigned a subject with which he is particularly
qualified to deal, as will be at once apparent even in this
preliminary announcement giving a list of some of the volumes in preparation.

ARRANGEMENT OF VOLUMES

A CRITICAL INTRODUCTION TO THE NEW TESTAMENT.
By ARTHUR SAMUEL PEAKE, D.D., Professor of Biblical Exegesis
and Dean of the Faculty of Theology, Victoria University, Man-
chester. Sometime Fellow of Merton College, Oxford. Author of
"A Guide to Biblical Study," "The Problem of Suffering in the
Old Testament," etc. *[Ready.*

FAITH AND ITS PSYCHOLOGY. By the Rev. WILLIAM R. INGE,
D.D., Lady Margaret Professor of Divinity, Cambridge, and
Bampton Lecturer, Oxford, 1899. Author of "Studies of the
English Mystics," "Truth and Falsehood in Religion," "Personal
Idealism and Mysticism," etc. *[Ready.*

PHILOSOPHY AND RELIGION. By the Rev. HASTINGS RASH-
DALL, D.Litt. (Oxon.), D.C.L. (Dunelm), F.B.A. Fellow and
Tutor of New College, Oxford. Author of "The Theory of Good
and Evil," etc., etc. *[Ready.*

REVELATION AND INSPIRATION. By the Rev. JAMES ORR, D.D., Professor of Apologetics in the Theological College of the United Free Church, Glasgow. Author of "The Christian View of God and the World," "The Ritschlian Theology and Evangelical Faith," "The Problem of the Old Testament," etc. *[Ready.*

CHRISTIANITY AND SOCIAL QUESTIONS. By the Rev. WILLIAM CUNNINGHAM, D.D., F.B.A., Fellow of Trinity College, Cambridge. Hon. Fellow of Gonville and Caius College, Cambridge. Archdeacon of Ely. Formerly Lecturer on Economic History to Harvard University. Author of "Growth of English History and Commerce," etc. *[Ready.*

CHRISTIAN THOUGHT TO THE REFORMATION. By HERBERT B. WORKMAN, D.Litt., Principal of the Westminster Training College. Author of "The Church of the West in the Middle Ages," "The Dawn of the Reformation," etc. *[Ready.*

PROTESTANT THOUGHT BEFORE KANT. By A. C. McGIFFERT, Ph.D., D.D., Professor of Church History in the Union Theological Seminary, New York. Author of "The History of Christianity in the Apostolic Age" and "The Apostles' Creed." *[Ready.*

THE CHRISTIAN HOPE: A STUDY IN THE DOCTRINE OF IMMORTALITY. By WILLIAM ADAMS BROWN, Ph.D., D.D., Professor of Systematic Theology in the Union Theological Seminary, New York. Author of "The Essence of Christianity" and "Christian Theology in Outline." *[Ready.*

HISTORY OF CHRISTIAN THOUGHT SINCE KANT. By the Rev. EDWARD CALDWELL MOORE, D.D., Parkman Professor of Theology in Harvard University. Author of "The New Testament in the Christian Church," etc. *[Ready.*

THE THEOLOGY OF THE GOSPELS. By the Rev. JAMES MOFFATT, D.D., D.Litt., Yates Professor of New Testament Greek and Exegesis, Mansfield College, Oxford. *[Ready.*

THE TEXT AND CANON OF THE NEW TESTAMENT. By ALEXANDER SOUTER, D.Litt. *[Ready.*

A HANDBOOK OF CHRISTIAN APOLOGETICS. By ALFRED ERNEST GARVIE, M.A., D.D. *[Ready.*

GOSPEL ORIGINS. By the Rev. WILLIAM WEST HOLDSWORTH, M.A.

Other volumes are in preparation and will be announced later.